THE HISTORY OF
CHOPPERS

{ ROLLING SCULPTURES }

THE HISTORY OF
CHOPPERS

{ ROLLING SCULPTURES }

R. Louis Wieland

Gibbs Smith, Publisher

ENRICH AND INSPIRE HUMANKIND

Salt Lake City | Charleston | Santa Fe | Santa Barbara

First Edition
11 09 08 07   5 4 3 2 1

Published by
Gibbs Smith, Publisher
P.O. Box 667
Layton, Utah 84041

Orders: 1.800.835.4993
www.gibbs-smith.com

Designed by Black Eye Design
Printed and bound in China

Library of Congress Cataloging-in-
Publication Data

Wieland, Rob.
  The history of choppers : rolling sculptures /
  R. Louis Wieland.—1st
ed.
    p. cm.
  ISBN-13: 978-1-58685-732-5
  ISBN-10: 1-58685-732-0
  1. Motorcycles—Customizing—United
States—History. 2. Motorcycling—United
States—History. I. Title.

TL439.5.U6W54 2007
629.227'5—dc22

2006030676

} TO DIANA, FOR LETTING ME BE IN THE RIGHT PLACE AT THE RIGHT TIME.

} TO MJR, FOR SLIDING THE TREASURE MAP UNDER THE DOOR AFTER OTHER PEOPLE CLOSED IT.

} TO DOUG, FOR MAKING IT ALL LOOK SO GOOD.

} TO LOUIE, FOR TEACHING ME THE MAGIC OF WORDS.

} AND, LIKE ALL BIKERS, I'VE GOT TO SHOW MY APPRECIATION TO MOM.

PHOTOGRAPH CREDITS

CONTENTS

THE MOTORCYCLE
MYTH

(BASIC BLACK, BUT NEVER OFF THE RACK.)

{"If I have to explain it,
you won't understand."}

T his is the first thing that most riders will say when asked, "What's it like to ride?" Some are a bit more eloquent. One owner said that every time he got on his bike it was like jumping onto "a steel rocket full of sex, drugs, and rock 'n' roll." Even riders who offer an explanation will tell you that words can't describe the feeling. There's a big pause, a couple of hand gestures, and a moment of thought. The uninitiated may not be able to understand, but for decades bikers have offered hundreds of bike styles to get their point across. Each of the bikes in this book is a mark of the builder's personality as surely as a signature is. It's an almost spiritual distinction. From the grungiest little dirt bike to the shiniest chrome sculpture on the street, motorcycles always turn heads and get noticed.

What makes the motorcycle myth ring true? It could be the primal feelings the rider gets from the wind in his (or her) face and the connection with the roadway. One of the first bits of biker slang I picked up was *cage*, an unflattering term used to describe automobiles. Driving a car is almost a passive experience. People apply makeup, chatter on cell phones, and toss down a bite to eat behind the wheel of a car. With the windows rolled up, the radio blaring, and the climate carefully controlled, it's easy to forget the vehicle is actually moving. On a motorcycle, these distractions are not an

option. Everything is right there within reach, and you could touch the highway. Bugs splatter themselves against *you*, not the windshield. The engine rumbles less than two feet away from your heart. Riding a motorcycle is as active as you can get on the highway. It's easy to see why riders get attached to their mounts.

The motorcycle myth also involves a connection to the past. While it's easy to see the similarities between bike riders and horse riders, the myth runs deeper. The world is still infatuated with the outlaw image that motorcycles have come to embody. For some, this myth is as big a selling point as horsepower and speed. A biker decked out in full leathers walking into a bar may as well be a gunslinger pushing

open the saloon doors. Everyone looking, many respect, some fear. It's no coincidence that the riding styles of motorcycles are descended from the saddles used by knights on horseback and cowboys on the range. The packs that many touring motorcycles use for luggage space are still called saddlebags. Not every rider thinks he is the next Marlon Brando or Wild Bill Hickok, but you'd be hard pressed to find someone who didn't mention a similar influence when he decided to learn to ride.

The place that choppers occupy in the motorcycle myth is one of a kind. In the modern era, you can't just point and click and order a 'factory custom' from a major motorcycle manufacturer. You can walk into a dealership and order a bike like you

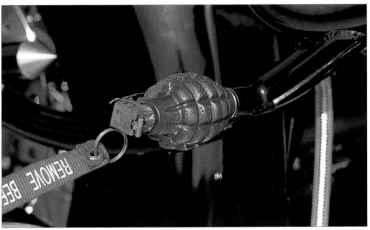

{THIS GEARSHIFT KNOB WAS MADE FROM AN ACTUAL DEACTI-
VATED HAND GRENADE.}

order a pizza. All it takes is a few days, a few bolt-on parts, and *presto*! Everyone likes to eat, but some folks love to cook. Choppers are to motorcycles what hot rods are to cars. Chopper riders and builders push that idea of self-expression even further, going past conveyance and into the realm of art. From the sleek lines of a custom job ordered by a movie star to the savage beauty of a rat bike put together from parts on hand, each of these bikes is unique. Whether outlaw or mainstream, the chopper has always been about self-expression and nonconformity: not working a 9-to-5, driving a 4-door, and living in a 3-bedroom. Sometimes it has meant pushing form over function; other times it has meant making do with what could be scrounged from a

junk pile. The modern chopper may have been born out of racing or removing unnecessary parts, but it quickly grew beyond that. None of the bikes here are ordinary and many are extraordinary. A few even go beyond extraordinary. Each one has a story, told by the color of the paint and the twist of the pipes. These stories are just as important as the history told here.

This book is a humble attempt to shed some light on this strange combination of sculpture, attitude, and individuality. Like any good living history, it's cobbled together from anecdotes, half-truths, a few facts, and many tall tales. It is just a gateway to a larger world that's getting easier to explore by the day thanks to the Internet and the current upswing in chopper popularity. It

is a chance to get a taste of biker culture without becoming bogged down by shop talk or tech specs. For experienced riders, there will be a story or two in this book that you've never heard and a chance to remember your own. The history of choppers could never be truly told in one volume. For every story you read here, ten more are being made on the road tonight. For every ten stories made on the road, there are a hundred experiences that words can't come close to expressing. It's tough writing a book about something you can't express in words. But the hard part's over. The next chapter is waiting to be written and the best place to start is on the road.

A Quiet Town Called Hollister

Hollister, California, had been hosting motorcycle events since the 1920s. With a location near Monterey Bay, it had become prime riding country. About one hundred miles south of San Francisco, Hollister was a scheduled stop on the American Motorcycle Association's "Gypsy Tour," a long ride through the countryside for members of the association. Of course, the AMA didn't expect twelve thousand people to show up for the first day of the event. According to the *San Francisco Chronicle* article written about the whole affair, state patrolmen were called in when around four thousand motorcyclists rolled into Hollister. It must have seemed like an invasion of black leather

Most of the mayhem had already ensued by the time the state troopers rolled in.

brigands akin to D-Day. Lieutenant Roy McPhail and his entire staff of seven lawmen panicked and called in the state troopers. The state troopers, led by Captain L. T. Torres, corralled the bikers into a one-block radius. No shots were fired, and nothing truly worthy of being called a riot happened. The cops even whistled up a band to play on the back of a flatbed truck for the motorcyclists.

Most of the mayhem had already ensued by the time the state troopers rolled in. Bottles littered the streets. The townsfolk had closed most of Main Street in response to the commotion in their quiet little town. Local bartenders stopped serving beer, hoping that the bikers couldn't afford whiskey. When that didn't work, the bars closed two hours before regular bar time. The local Legion Hall cancelled the scheduled party, but admittedly, the party was already taking place right there on Main Street.

The cops themselves didn't do a good job of keeping the peace. Herding a few thousand people and their bikes into the space of a couple blocks is a quick way to put a crowd into a pressure cooker. Some of the bikers were none too pleased at being treated like

{CHOPPERS ARE MEANT TO
LOOK GOOD ON THE SIDE OF
THE ROAD . . . }

{. . . OR IN A PHOTOGRA-
PHER'S STUDIO.}

cattle. They preened and prodded, but no violence directed at the police ever materialized. Several hundred bikers did spend the night on the courthouse lawn; how many of these campers were demonstrating civil disobedience and how many simply lacked lodging is a question lost to the ages.

Hollister saw its population nearly double over that fateful July Fourth weekend. Skittish cops arrested as many of the unruly bikers as they could. The bikers pushed back by holding races on the streets; the local hospital became overloaded with bikers who didn't have enough room to ride safely. Each side did a little something to push the other side just a bit. By the Fourth of July, a full-blown riot easily could have broken out. Instead, a handful of bikers were busted on small-time charges like indecent exposure, public drunkenness, and disturbing the peace.

The real reason for the riot at Hollister was not the surly disposition of the riders at the outset. But throw a party without enough refreshments, places to stay, and things to do, and guests are bound to make their own fun. Of course, when people are left to their own devices, the fun is usually not for the whole family. When a

{THE THROWBACK SPEEDOMETER IS A PERFECT EXAMPLE OF THE HISTORY OF BIKE PARTS.}

{THIS JET-BLACK RACER SAYS NO THANKS TO CHROME PIPES.}

{WHILE THE HANDLEBARS AND FARING ARE OLD SCHOOL. . .}

{THE REGAL PURPLE DRAWS EVEN MORE ATTENTION.}

{AIR SCOOPS HELP THE ENGINE COOL MORE QUICKLY.}

{SHORT PIPES ARE LOUD PIPES.}

{THE PULL-BACK HANDLE-
BARS ARE A NECESSITY ON A
DESIGN LIKE THIS.}

riot mentality takes hold, things go downhill quickly.

However, what happened at Hollister soon entered the realm of urban legend. Figures were misreported. Stories were embellished. Word of mouth painted a rowdier picture than the events back up. People preferred a good story to something as boring as the facts and ate it up. Soon enough, riders were getting suspicious looks when they pulled into service stations. The AMA began to distance itself from the events of Hollister. The indignant cries of the participants were drowned out by moral pronouncements against these new-fangled bikers, now branded as public nuisances in America's mind.

A Wild Story

The idea of the biker as an outlaw was not really cultivated until after World War II. While some groups of riders raised hell and gave local law enforcement gray hairs, they were no different from any other rowdy groups that came into town, like hot-rodders or rock 'n' roll musicians. The corporate motorcycle clubs also did their part to encourage people to toe the line. In fact, the term *outlaw gang* originally meant a gang of bikers that wasn't affiliated with a corporate club or the AMA. The sensational tales told about the Hollister rally started to push the image of motorcycling into

Biker characters soon became a favorite choice of villain in Hollywood.

outlaw territory. The staged picture was worth a thousand words of condemnation. However, one event in 1953 really solidified the outlaw motorcycle image forever. In that year, a film originally titled *Hot Blood* was released. When the advertisers decided to feature handsome young Marlon Brando after his success in *A Streetcar Named Desire*, the title of the film was changed to *The Wild One*.

The movie is based on "The Cyclists's Raid," a short story written for *Harper's Magazine* in 1951. The story was a fictionalization of the Hollister event. The movie features Brando and Lee Marvin as the heads of rival motorcycle gangs. In the film, Brando's Black Rebels Motorcycle Club steals a trophy from a legitimate motorcycle club race. They end up in the nearby town of Wrightsville, where they cow the local sheriff into submission and set up shop in the local watering hole. Brando's Johnny starts to fall for the waitress when in rides Lee Marvin leading the Beetles. The two gangs clash when their showdown on Main Street overturns a car and frightens the townsfolk. Lee Marvin's character is sent to jail. The

gangs continue to terrorize the small town until Johnny falls for the girl and starts to redeem himself. He gives up his rivalry, his gang, and even the girl, for a chance to start fresh again on his own. With Johnny came the birth of the "bad boy with a heart of gold" character, now a classic archetype alongside the good guy in the white hat. James Dean and Elvis built their public personas on this archetype, and they benefited from it immensely. Biker characters soon became a favorite choice of villain in Hollywood. It doesn't take much imagination to turn the war whoop of the American Indian antagonists of western films into the roar of a motorcycle as bikers rumble into town.

The Wild One caused quite a sensation when it came out. It was banned in Great Britain for nearly fifteen years. Opponents often decried it as communist for glamorizing youthful rebellion against good old America. Marlon Brando's persona, with his black leather jacket, his hat tipped to the side, and his defiant sneer fixed on anyone radiating authority, changed the youth of America. For every businessman who was put off by the film, there were five kids slicking their hair, rolling up their sleeves, and bobbing whatever bikes they could get their hands on. Owning a bike soon became an instant ticket to a bad reputation. *Harley* soon became a negative term thrown at any young man who looked too much like a rebel. Motorcycles soon became synonymous with another taboo of the time: sex. Girls who liked men who rode motorcycles were obviously of easy virtue. Even though the images on Harley advertisements were of clean-cut kids, when most folks heard the rumble of a motorcycle they thought of modern-day Mongols ransacking the town.

The two motorcycle gangs in the film offered young men two rebellious role models. Marvin's Chino was brash, loud-mouthed, and dirty. Brando's Johnny was slick, sexy, and troubled. But the movie made important cultural mistakes. Johnny's band of rebels rode Harleys, while Chino's gang rode Triumphs. Most of the outlaw gangs fictionalized by the film wouldn't be caught dead on the sportier Triumphs. The gangs themselves thought it was a joke; the head of the San Francisco Hell's Angels, Frank Salidek, bought the shirt that Lee Marvin wore in the movie and wore it only when he met with police officials. A lot of the gangs at the time were made up of WWII veterans, not the teenage lads who followed Johnny around. The lesson to be learned was one of perceptions.

The bobber community learned that lesson the hard way. As every Tom, Dick, and Harry picked up a bike to play Brando on the weekends, the older, more experienced riders needed to do things to pull away from

{JOHNNY WOULD APPRECIATE THIS BIKE WITH ITS CLASSIC FLAME MOTIF AND HARD TAIL SEAT.}

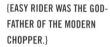
{A DUAL EXHAUST TELLS EVERYONE THAT YOU DON'T CARE HOW LOUD YOUR BIKE IS.}

the pack. They started altering their bikes, not because they were going to be hip-deep in mud or running hill climbs but because they wanted the weekend warriors to know they had been around since the beginning. Instead of just ripping things off, they began to weld things on. Form was becoming just as important as function. These changes started the evolution from the bobber to the chopper.

This era of bikers on film came to a close with *The Wild Angels*, a film directed by the notorious Roger Corman about the Hell's Angels. The film was released in 1968 and actually featured the outlaw gang cooperating with the filmmakers. It tells the story of a gang member who tries to steal a bike from the cops after his own bike is stolen. The gang member is shot and caught. The gang tries to bust him out of the hospital, but he dies in the process. This film updated the look of the bad guy biker for the late 1960s and cemented the rowdy, sinful associations by showing the bikers participating in drugs, rape, and a variety of other illegal activities. Interestingly, the starring role in this film was played by Peter Fonda, whose next project was *Easy Rider*.

Born to Be Wild

The year 1969 changed everything. Because they originated in the same part of the world, choppers and hippie culture became linked. The outlaw gangs that existed on the fringe of society stood shoulder to shoulder with the communes that rebelled against the straights. These revolutions rolled through American culture like an avalanche, knocking down civil rights, music, and dozens of other traditional ideas. The revolution hit film with the 1969 release of *Easy Rider*.

Easy Rider changed both the face and focus of motorcycling. Peter Fonda and Dennis Hopper replaced Brando and Elvis. The film centers on the journey made by two bikers through America. It's a bleak

{EASY RIDER WAS THE GOD-FATHER OF THE MODERN CHOPPER.}

look at the aftermath of the Summer of Love and the polarization of society at the time. The tagline for the movie was "A man went looking for America and couldn't find it anywhere." The film was a reflection of the times: the riders take a trip through a commune, some famous western scenery, a drug deal, and a parade, and finally come to a bleak ending where the shotgun-wielding rednecks kill the protagonists. While Captain America and Billy don't find America, it hunts them down at the end.

The film's star, Fonda, draped himself in flag imagery. He spent a week breaking in the bike and often found himself on the side of the road as policemen pulled him over for his long hair and strange looking motorcycle. Hopper was rumored to have taken his character of a paranoid, delusional hippie much too far into the real world. Jack Nicholson starred as a prison-mate lawyer, symbolic of the establishment, which liked to slum around with the hippies while condemning them on high. The grass that was

{THE TANK WAS SCULPTED TO MIRROR THE THORAX OF AN INSECT.}

{WHILE THE RED PAINT MAY BE CLASSIC, THE SCALE-LIKE PATTERN GIVES THIS BIKE LIFE.}

{THE FAT RACER TIRE LETS THE RIDER PUT MORE RUBBER ON THE GROUND.}

smoked on-screen was real. The Mardi Gras scenes were shot on location without permission from the City of New Orleans, and the damage done to the crypts resulted in a long-standing ban of commercial filming within city limits. The film was raw and unique, not unlike the bikes that rode out of the movie screen and into the imaginations of Americans.

Like many trends in the '60s, the chopper movement was pushed to excess. Everything became bigger, longer, faster, and more dangerous. The evolution of motorcycle from workhorse to artwork was nearing completion.

{BILLY AND WYATT'S BIKES HAVE BECOME TWO OF THE MOST POPULAR SKELETONS FOR BUILDING INNOVATIVE BIKES.}

The True Red, White, and Blue Chopper

{THE FUNCTIONING BIKES WERE STOLEN SHORTLY AFTER THE END OF PRODUCTION.}

Today, when people think of choppers, chances are they imagine a bike like the one ridden by Peter Fonda's Captain America. Fonda was an experienced motorcyclist and had the bike custom built for *Easy Rider*. Four bikes were built for the film, but only one survives today. The other three were stolen, and their whereabouts have become something of an urban legend among bike builders. Most builders believe the bikes were busted up for spare parts, meaning that dozens of bikes have pieces of the legendary choppers.

The Captain is the perfect example of a chopper because it stands out from stock bikes; it's eye-catching compared to other custom bikes as well. The process begins with the removal of everything that might be considered unnecessary to lighten up the bike and make it go faster. While parts like the front fender and seat springs are at the top of the list, other items, like front brakes and turn signals, often find themselves on the scrap heap as well. If the bike still runs, strip it off. The Captain America bike is a perfect example of this philosophy. The front fender was one of the first casualties, since this bike isn't going through any mud soon. It lacks front brakes because the rear ones will do just as well. No seat springs mean you can feel the vibration of the bike as well as every bump in the road. This is amplified by the lack of a suspension, since the sleek lines leaves no room for shock absorbers. The windshield is unnecessary because half the fun of riding is feeling the wind in your hair. Turn signals are for squares, man.

It was the beginning of an era of excess in bikes and in the world. Just like collars and hairdos, the chopper would swell to epic proportions.

One of the most unusual features about the bike is its abundance of chrome. While many custom builders chromed some parts of the motorcycle, the builder of the Captain America chromed the majority of its surfaces. Even the rear fender was chromed, with a passenger seat attached to it. Maintaining the bike's good looks was quite a chore, since many of the parts that took day-to-day abuse were chromed.

Another interesting feature is the headlights, which were often one of the first things to go on a custom bike. But this model kept them. In theory, this was because the film crew was shooting at night, but it provides a perfect example of the rules of chopper building: there aren't any.

The ape hanger handlebars are an interesting instance of form over function. Front-set pegs and handlebars make riding more comfortable because the rider can stretch out his limbs for long rides, but these ape hangers are stretched above and beyond the norm.

Another feature of the bike that really turned heads was the sheer volume of American flag imagery. We live in blatantly patriotic times, but in the 1960s, plastering the American flag all over everything was rebellious. In a movie that depicted America's counterculture in such a detailed manner, this caused controversy akin to making a movie about communism starring George Washington.

Depending on whom you ask, *Easy Rider* was a movie about what was going on in America at the time, or it was the first sign that the counterculture was selling out. The movie brought choppers into the mainstream and brought back the dangerous beauty of the outlaws and their bikes. It was the beginning of an era of excess in bikes and in the world. Just like collars and hairdos, the chopper would swell to epic proportions. The bike would get

Outstanding choppers aren't made, they're born. Born in the imagination of the chopper builder long before the bike becomes a finished reality.

The flair of imagination is really what makes a truly outstanding chopper. John Wiseman, Karl Lindner, and Bob Steuwer have outstanding choppers. Outstanding because they were built with imagination,

craftsmanship, and the finest parts available. These chopper builders chose parts that excited their imaginations. Parts that were crafted with the same care, quality and imagination that they put into their own machines. These builders chose A.E.E. parts.

Turn on your imagination with A.E.E. Send for the all new CHOPPER GUIDE and find out

what other people's imaginations are up to and let your imagination run wild with the newest A.E.E. parts and accessories. Send $1.95 to A.E.E. CHOPPERS, INC., Dept. 5C, 730 Monroe Way, Placentia, California 92670.

OUTSTANDING CHOPPERS: IMAGINATION PLUS A.E.E.

{MANY PARTS VENDORS OFFERED KITS TO BUILD THE BIKES FEATURED IN THE FILM.}

pushed out of the realm of the rideable and into the realm of sculpture. And just like disco, it was all headed for a very big fall.

The Man Who Put the Devil in Daredevil

The cinema helped to romanticize the outlaw biker as well as the chopper. As the idea of the biker as modern desperado became more common, the outlaw biker image was drawn into the mainstream. Droves of *Easy Rider* fans fantasized about riding choppers across the country. But then a different kind of biker took America by storm. While choppers pushed the appearance of bikes, this rider pushed the performance of bikes. He was born Robert Craig Knievel Jr., but kids born in the '70s knew him as Evel Knievel.

Knievel first came into contact with daredevils as a boy. At the age of eight, he attended a Joie Chitwood Auto Daredevil show, an experience that influenced his decision to become one himself. He got into trouble a lot as a teenager. This wild-child reputation earned him his famous name. After crashing his motorcycle during a police chase in 1956, Knievel was taken to jail on a charge of reckless driving. When the night jailer came around to check the roll, he said, "Hey, we got a guy named Knievel in one cell and another named Knofel in the other. Goddamn! Double the guard! We got Evil Knievel and Awful Knofel here tonight." The nickname stuck.

Knievel took to being a daredevil as a last resort. Before jumping motorcycles for a living, he worked as a soldier, a hockey player, a game hunter, an insurance salesman, and even a Honda dealer. He found moderate success as a motocross rider but his injuries kept him from a regular schedule. Remembering the daredevils he had seen as a child, he put together his first daredevil jump. After showing off with a few wheelies and other tricks, he jumped over a twenty-foot box of rattlesnakes and a pair of mountain lions.

Fonzie's allure was that he was cool, tough, confident, independent, arrogant, and above all, dominated by no one.

{KNIEVEL AWAKENED A LOT OF BOYS TO THE LURE OF BIKES}

While the landing wasn't perfect, he stayed upright and found his niche.

He did all the work for the first jump himself: finding a venue, writing press releases, and even selling tickets. Then he found a sponsor and hired a staff so he could concentrate on the jumps. His newly assembled show experienced some success in California, but, conscious of the outlaw biker image, he changed the spelling of his nickname from "Evil" to "Evel" on the sign to read "Evel Knievel and His Motorcycle Daredevils."

Predictably, injuries plagued Knievel throughout his career. But his crashes were just as important as his successful jumps. National TV covered his attempt to jump the fountains at Caesar's Palace in Las Vegas. The public embraced his refusal to stay down. Knievel embodied the outlaw spirit of the biker while engaging in activities that could be shown on color TV. By this time, he was making $25,000 per jump, but he wanted more. Bigger and

better jumps were one way to do it, but his injuries reminded him that he wouldn't be around forever.

He realized the big money was in merchandising. Young boys around the country watched his feats on Saturday afternoons, thanks to television. They grew up idolizing him and his desire to make more dangerous jumps. The same kids that were riding chopper bicycles had Evel Knievel bed sheets.

The Fonz

With the outlaw spirit of motorcycles for sale, the last step in turning the biker from outlaw to hero came from, of all places, Milwaukee. The perfect example of America's love-hate relationship with the image of the biker comes from an ABC series that presented television's only long-running biker character. The show was called *Happy Days* and the character was Arthur Fonzarelli, nicknamed the Fonz. Though Fonzie was initially a minor character, he soon blossomed into a popular phenomenon. It was yet another example of Hollywood villainizing and romanticizing motorcycles at the same time. Fonzie started out as a bad kid to contrast with the squeaky-clean family in the foreground. But America loves an underdog hero, and Fonzie soon became the breakout character of the series.

Fonzie's allure was that he was cool, tough, confident, independent, arrogant, and above all, dominated by no one. The Fonz was also likable and not a real threat. He would always step in to save the day and only got into fights with guys that swung first. He was unique in that he was one of the first anti-heroes to populate a sitcom. Fonzie filled the role of worldly foil to Richie Cunningham's innocence. For much of the program's ten-year run, Fonzie advised Richie and his pals, instructing them in the ways of the world, acting as a measuring stick for their own development as men, and bailing them out when they failed to meet the standard.

Acting as a working-class touchstone, the Fonz passed on his hard-earned knowledge and experience to Richie. Coming out of the biker myth, he was most apt to show them the value of courage and self-reliance. But the Fonz also handed out moral lessons about honesty and friendship, and he was, oddly enough, an early example of political correctness. He brought African Americans into the Cunningham household, worked with the handicapped, dated a deaf woman, and for one episode dealt with his own blindness. If not for Fonzie's intervention, Richie's education would have been incomplete.

Fonzie was, then, a way for the Cunninghams, and by extension the viewing audience, to temporarily commune with a lifestyle they had never experienced or had lost touch with. This social education and middle-class critique by way of biker outlaws and motorcycles remains popular in sitcoms. Even before the rebirth of the Harley-Davidson as the

{FAST FORWARD A FEW YEARS AND THE FONZ EASILY COULD HAVE TURNED INTO A CHOP-PER RIDER.}

icon of freedom and independence, motorcycles symbolized "forbidden fruit" to otherwise stable middle-class and professional sitcom characters. Hit shows such as *The Bob Newhart Show*, *Roseanne*, and *Married with Children* ran episodes in which a main male character picks up a bike to explore that same outlaw image. In each case, the character becomes frustrated in his attempt to escape the workaday world, the motorcycle becomes a complication in his life, and the only way to return to stability is to sell it.

The Nicest People

In 1962, the American motorcycle market was crowded. British bikes like the Norton and the Triumph were competing for the youth market and for speed-oriented bikers (as opposed to touring bikers). Japanese bikes had entered the fray as well, with Honda selling more than forty thousand motorcycles annually. The company had set up more than 750 dealerships in the U.S. It had the largest number of dealers in the country. Then Honda upped the ante. For 1963, it wanted it's dealers to sell two hundred thousand bikes. While the competition gawked and laughed, the management at Honda had a plan. They knew that motorcycles were popular among the young and the rebellious. The trick was to expand the market and bring fresh faces into the dealerships. By bringing motorcycling into the mainstream, the company could meet its ambitious sales goals and make money hand over fist against established names like Harley-Davidson. Honda decided to run an ad campaign aimed in eleven western states and hired Grey Advertising to come up with a plan that would accomplish something new. Rather than touting the free-wheeling image of motorcycles, the ad campaign reintroduced motorcycles as a low-cost, casual alternative to automobiles. The slogan

{WHILE THE COMPANY ITSELF MAY OFFICIALLY DISTANCE ITS BIKES FROM CHOPPERS, MANY BUILDERS USE ITS PARTS AS ESSENTIAL COMPONENTS.}

quickly became unforgettable, both to suburban dwellers who bought into it and to the hard-core bikers who muttered it under their breath whenever they saw a Honda putter by.

The "You Meet the Nicest People on a Honda" campaign depicted young couples, parents and children, policemen, grocery-getting housewives, and other respectable members of society riding Honda motorcycles. The colorful illustration and highly professional design put the competition to shame. The ads showed these upright citizens zooming out to the grocers, the ball game, and the beach. The smiling faces and oh-so-white teeth converted a whole new segment of motorcyclists. Parents who would have sent their son to a military school if they found out he was interested in motorcycles compromised by buying Hondas. The Honda 50 became a popular present for

birthdays and Christmas. With support from students, housewives, businessmen, and outdoor enthusiasts, the motorcycle finally won recognition as a popular product. The real bikers and chopper builders laughed and shrugged it off . . . at first.

The professionals at Grey Advertising could see how well the campaign was going. They could feel public perception of motorcycles turning, and they knew they had to strike while the iron was hot. So the advertising firm suggested that Honda buy two ad segments during the *Academy Awards*. The spots would cost $300,000, which was the revenue from 1,200 Honda 50s. But the agency maintained that these spots would reach from seventy to eighty percent of all television viewers. It was a big gamble, but it could pay off big. The ads would put the Honda name and product line out in front of America and try to shake off more than a decade of negative public perception. The executives at Honda nervously agreed. American Honda became the first foreign corporation to sponsor the *Academy Awards* show. No one had ever heard of a motor-cycle company sponsoring the event, and both the motorcycle industry and the media took notice.

The response was simply overwhelming. Additional commercials followed, and Hondas became a sensation across the country. New dealer inquiries poured in every day. Honda's big dealership network became gargantuan. Corporations across the U.S. began to inundate American Honda with inquiries concerning tie-ins and promotions. The Honda 50 in particular had truly succeeded in its appeal to the American public. By playing against type, it was seen as a casual vehicle for daily activities, and as such was a hit with an entirely new consumer. In addition to turning heads, the bikes were cheap and easy to maintain. The image of Brando and his cocked leather hat was buried under V-neck sweaters and college boys.

But the expanding motorcycle market also signaled the beginning of the true chopper era, as builders discontented with all the Johnny-come-lately Honda riders searched for ways to really push the envelope and set themselves apart from the Nicest People. Strangely, the birthplace of this movement, the western U.S., was also where the strands of the chopper's DNA were just starting to come together.

{NOWADAYS, YOU MEET THE NICEST PEOPLE ON BIKES LIKE THIS.}

{BELL BOTTOMS WERE AS IMPORTANT TO SOME RIDERS AS ORGAN PIPES.}

A CHOPPER IS
BORN

{In the beginning}

In the beginning so much excitement surrounds a machine that was born as an accident—the happy result of early attempts to refine the internal combustion engine. It's often the case with technological innovations; no one person can take sole credit for the invention of the motorcycle. In the process of developing an air-cooled, four-stroke engine for automotive use, Gottlieb Daimler (who later teamed up with Karl Benz to form the Daimler-Benz Corporation) constructed a petrol-powered bicycle in 1885. Within a few years they appeared in large numbers in France and Germany, and by 1896 these contraptions, flitting about at a top speed of about 24 mph, had taken on the familiar shape of the modern motorcycle. Those early machines were, after all, noisy and uncomfortable, and the engines were especially sensitive to every bounce and jiggle. Every trip was an adventure. Like many inventions of the industrial age, the motorcycle was worked on from many different angles at the same time. Motorcycle history scholars can't decide where the first true motorcycle comes from.

Motorcycles are descended from "safety" bicycles—those with front and rear wheels of the same size with a pedal crank mechanism to drive the rear wheel. Those bicycles, in turn, were descended from high-wheel bicycles. The high-wheelers were descendants of an early type of pushbike without pedals, propelled by the rider's feet pushing against the ground. These appeared around 1800, used iron-banded wagon wheels, and were called "bone-crushers," both for their jarring ride and their tendency to toss their riders.

Gottlieb Daimler's 1885 motorbike had one wheel in the front and one in the back, although it had a smaller spring-loaded outrigger wheel on each side. It was constructed mostly of wood, with iron-banded wooden-spoke wagon-type wheels, definitely a bone-crusher chassis. It was powered by a single-cylinder Otto-cycle engine, and may have had a spray-type carburetor. Spray carburetors are called such because they expel directly to the ground. Daimler's assistant was working on the invention of the spray carburetor at the time.

If you consider two wheels with steam propulsion a motorcycle, then the first one may have been American. Sylvester Howard Roper of Roxbury, Massachusetts,

built a steam-powered machine called a "velocipede" in 1867. He exhibited it at various fairs and circuses along the eastern seaboard. It's powered by a charcoal-fired two-cylinder engine, whose connecting rods directly drive a crank on the rear wheel. This machine predates the invention of the safety bicycle by many years, so its chassis is also based on the bone-crusher bike. Most of the development during this era concentrated on three- and four-wheeled designs, since it was complex enough to get the machines running without having to worry about them falling over. The next really notable two-wheeler was the Millet of 1892.

{CHOPPER BUILDERS OFTEN USE DIFFERENT WHEEL SIZES ON THE SAME BIKE.}

{THE LOW SEATS LET A RIDER SIT FOR LONG DISTANCES WITH STRAIGHT LEGS.}

It used a 5-cylinder engine built as the hub of its rear wheel. The cylinders rotated with the wheel, and its crankshaft constituted the rear axle.

The first really successful production two-wheeler was the Hildebrand & Wolfmueller, patented in Munich in 1894. It had a step-through frame, with its fuel tank mounted on the downtube. It used a parallel-twin engine, mounted low on the frame, with fore and aft cylinders. The connecting rods connected directly to a crank on the rear axle, and instead of using heavy flywheels for energy storage between cylinder firing, it used a pair of stout elastic bands, one on each side outboard of the cylinders, to help with the compression strokes. It was water-cooled, with a water tank/radiator built into the top of the rear fender.

In 1895, the French firm of DeDion-Buton built an engine that made the mass production and common use of motorcycles possible. It was a small, light, high-revving, four-stroke single, and used battery-and-coil ignition, doing away with the troublesome hot-tube. Bore and stroke figures of 50mm by 70mm gave a displacement of 138cc. A total loss lubrication system dripped oil into the crankcase through a metering valve, and the oil sloshed around to lubricate and cool components before dripping to the

{A HUNDRED MILES ON THE
RAZOR'S EDGE.}

Motorcycles were also not for the faint-hearted. Early riders earned their reputations as iron men. In return, motorcycles provided a very special delight that combined the intimacy of horseback riding with the speed of an automobile. Nobody cared that the over-powered bicycles were temperamental, noisy, dirty, painful, and completely antisocial—they were fun.

During the first two decades of the twentieth century, technical innovations redeemed some of the least appealing aspects of cycling. Up to that point, riders pedaled or ran alongside their bikes to get them started. Because of the cycle's low

{THIS IS A LONG WAY FROM A STEAM ENGINE.}

ground via a breather. DeDion-Buton used this 1/2-horsepower powerplant in road-going trikes, but the engine was copied and used by everybody, including Indian and Harley-Davidson in the U.S.

Although a gentleman named Jonas "Airship" Pennington built some machines around 1895 (it's uncertain whether any of them actually ran), the first U.S. production motorcycle was the Orient-Aster, built by the Metz Company in Waltham, Massachusetts, in 1898. It used an Aster engine that was a French-built copy of the DeDion-Buton, and predated Indian (1901) by three years, and Harley-Davidson (1902) by four. Its fickle temperament may have been the machine's saving grace. Early motorcycles demanded great dedication and mechanical skill of their riders. Those first-generation bikers were up to the task, though, since they were often the machine's designers and builders, well aware of its moods and limitations.

{ TO CHOPPER BUILDERS, THE LOOK
IS JUST AS IMPORTANT AS THE RIDE. }

power, riders often had to jump off and push them up hills. In addition, too many manufacturers, too few mechanics, and too many designs hampered the industry. When a small four-stroke engine replaced the bottom bracket on the standard safety bicycle frame, the motorcycle's future brightened. This design improved the motorcycle's balance by lowering the center of gravity and better distributing the weight of engine and rider.

Both rider and machine changed during the early 1900s. A new type of man took up motorcycling. The iron men became the minority, replaced by those looking for utility. To that end, between 1905 and 1915, practically every modern motorcycle design

During the first two decades of the twentieth century, technical innovations redeemed some of the least appealing aspects of cycling.

feature appeared: spring forks for comfort; handlebar controls for mixing oil, fuel, and air; improved dynamos for starting and lighting; V-belts and an occasional chain drive; and fat tires that could be repaired and changed in a matter of minutes rather than hours. What most folks would consider a motorcycle took shape. The look of an engine bolted onto a bicycle frame quickly fell away.

With this semblance of standardization and organization came the necessity of racing, the tests of speed and endurance and of the rider's skills. Prior to 1903, a handful of men occasionally gathered at horse tracks and bicycle velodromes to race their

{THIS TANK GOES FOR THAT "BOLTED-ON" LOOK.}

machines at speeds in excess of 30 mph. In this country, 1903 saw the formation of the Federation of American Motorcyclists (FAM), which in 1908 put together its first organized event, a two-day endurance run around New York City and Long Island. The president of the Harley-Davidson Motor Company, Walter Davidson, mounted an early Harley to defeat eighty-four other riders representing twenty-two different makes of motorcycle.

The first Harley-Davidson had rolled out of the one-room Milwaukee machine shop operated by Bill and Walter Davidson and William Harley in 1903. A year earlier, the first Indian motorcycle sprang out

{NOWADAYS, MOST CHOPPER BUILDERS USE FIBERGLASS TO GET THEIR FRAMES TO DEFY GRAVITY.}

{IN MANY WAYS, THE CHOPPER IS A RETURN TO THE DAYS WHEN THE RIDER BUILT THE MACHINE BY HAND.}

of Springfield, Massachusetts. These two manufacturers, along with Henderson and Excelsior, would come to define motorcycling in the United States and reign over racing and endurance contests early in the century. Harley-Davidson's famed Wrecking Crew dominated the sport between 1916 and 1921. But 1921 also saw sales of Harley-Davidsons slump, prompting the company to pull out of racing. The FAM itself had collapsed in 1919, replaced in 1923 by the American Motorcyclists Association (AMA).

The Wrecking Crew

The era of the chopper did not begin on a specific date like a war or the reign of a king. While motorcycle makers at the turn of the century began their businesses in shacks, garages, and basements, motorcycles became a bustling industry in the ensuing years. More than three hundred motorcycle manufacturers in America alone sprung up in the first twenty years of the twentieth century. While the giants like Harley-Davidson and Indian quickly began to establish themselves and their rivalries, a handful of other companies took their shots as well.

{THIS BIKE MAY BE GRAY, BUT IT SURE ISN'T SILENT . . . }

The motorcycle had a charmed childhood alongside its four-wheeled brother, the automobile. During this time, America was still largely rural. The big cities remained near the waterways. While the rail had conquered the West, interstate highways were still a fantasy. Rural roads were rutted and muddy, and city streets were not much better. Modeled after European cities, many urban centers in the U.S. had narrow, cobbled streets, which made travel difficult in any vehicle. Automobiles, still a luxury, could be loud, unreliable, and dangerous. Motorcycles were seen as a cheaper alternative to cars. They could go more places and do more things. The big companies began to exploit this in their advertising. During this period, Harley-Davidson called its motorcycles "The Silent Gray Fellows" and crowed about how quiet and efficient they were compared to the rattling claptraps manufactured in Detroit.

Motor sports evolved along similar lines. People would gather for a variety of events that were forerunners of modern motocross. Many companies sponsored their own racing and event teams. Not only was it great press, it was an excellent way to demonstrate the features of the motorcycles. Of course, operating comparatively unreliable machines at high speeds made motocross a dangerous occupation. The teams were sometimes called "Wrecking Crews," and it is in their company we find another piece of the chopper's early history.

Companies provided their crews with stock machines, but racers didn't keep them that way for long. In addition to the usual tweaks, improvements, and experiments, mechanics often had to effect repairs from materials on hand. If a team was racing the state fair circuit, waiting for official parts on order took time better spent on the actual repair work.

But the racing circuit did not last. By 1919, motorcycle sales had dropped considerably. As the 1920s began to roar, America made the automobile its vehicle of choice. The motorcycle slipped to a distant second as the car overcame its shortcomings and popped up in garages across the country. Hundreds of motorcycle manufacturers now faltered and withered. Even the composition of motorcycle ridership changed as motorcycling became essentially a man's hobby.

Depression and Delinquency

The AMA sanctioned nearly three hundred motorcycle clubs in the 1930s but membership declined amid Depression hardships. Clubs became a subculture, with members wearing clothes available only from a motorcycle dealer. Rather than the leathers and denim we know today, the outfits were right out of the marching band catalog, complete with strange hats and jodhpurs. These clubs, however, represented the responsible riders. They had strict dress codes, and members wore military-style uniforms. Yet they were (and still are to some extent) overlooked when people thought of bikers. AMA clubs promoted responsible motorcycling as a family activity. Organized clubs sponsored mixers, charity events, races, and hill-climbing contests.

The period following World War II was characterized by a variety of threats to the middle-class family. Changes in youth culture inspired confusion and fear in older Americans unprepared and unwilling to accept such rapid social change. The result was hostility and suspicion between

{COMPANY-SPONSORED CLUBS FEATURED UNIFORMS AND SPIFFY MODELS IN THEIR CATALOGS.}

{THE RIDER MUST PRESS HIS BODY AGAINST THE TANK TO REACH THE HANDLEBARS OF THIS BIKE.}

{CHOPPERS LIKE THIS ARE BUILT FOR MAXIMUM SPEED. NOTE THE "DRAGSTER" FRAME.}

generations, and the belief that teenagers had somehow lost their moral bearings. In the postwar world, the changing behavior of youth in terms of speech, fashions, music, and mores, appeared to erase the boundaries between hijinks and premature adulthood and even delinquency. Taken together, events of the era validated increased concern as well as increased expenditures for adolescent counseling, education, and law enforcement.

The 1950s painted a friendlier, if no less disconcerting, portrait of America. Conformity and materialism were the rule, and deviance came at a pretty price. The rise of McDonald's fast-food restaurants, Holiday Inns, and television sitcoms created a society resistant to and increasingly intolerant of nonconformists, free spirits, and rebels. The Beats, exemplified by Jack Kerouac and Allen Ginsberg, looked outside the system for freedom. The growing youth culture that idolized Marlon Brando, Elvis Presley, and James Dean identified with being misunderstood, especially by parents. Blandness and a spirit of conformity mixed with a lack of serious social and cultural purpose marked middle-class life in America, and those with the temerity to turn their backs on it were the pioneers of the following decade's counterculture.

Perceptions of increased delinquency, the growing popularity of rock-and-roll

Photos by Billy Tinney

{THESE RIDERS BROUGHT ABOUT THE DECLINE OF WESTERN CIVILIZATION.}

music and hot-rodding, the new social mobility and economic independence of adolescents, and changing definitions of right and wrong dovetailed with the older generation's Cold War hysteria and fear of anarchy and conspiracy. Social tensions mounted. Criminologists blamed the moral breakdown on global tensions; the only cure was a stiffening of the moral fabric of the nation and a spiritual renaissance.

Most disturbing was the potential for violence by future generations of suburban teens. With fathers spending too much time at work, society would create isolated homes and emotionally starved children. In too many homes, the mother

{THE COFFIN TANK AND THE CORPORATE LOGO ARE AN INTERESTING COMBINATION.}

{THE RUMBLES OF ENGINES COULD SHAKE UP AN ENTIRE TOWN.}

was too busy with an eternal round of social activities to have any real relationship with her children. The result would be unhappiness in the midst of plenty. Where mothers took charge of the home, boys rebelled and displayed extreme masculine attitudes, violence, and even sadism.

Rootlessness, mobility, and a burgeoning population also figured into the equation. Americans were on the move. People of many ethnic groups and cultural backgrounds poured into places like California and New York. This heavy population resulted in friction between the newcomers and old-timers.

Cars and motorcycles provided one outlet for alienated young men and motorheads who felt unfairly constrained, isolated, or just out of place in postwar America. In hot-rod culture, with its roots running as far back as the Model T, a kid bought a stock automobile and tinkered until he had the most unique machine possible, one that would reflect who he was or who he wanted to be. If he could shut down someone else's rod, all the better.

{CHOPPERS AND HARLEYS OFTEN OCCUPY THE SAME FAMILY TREE.}

Similarly, Harley-Davidsons attracted men and boys who wanted to express themselves mechanically but could not afford an automobile. The bikes were familiar to World War II vets, and they were rugged and fairly cheap. With a bit of work they could also be quite fast. But even more important for later generations of cyclists, the Harley 74 (74 cubic inches), the bike of choice for the early outlaw clubs, was easy to repair and easy to personalize. Harleys were revered by motorcycle clubs because they could be stripped down to their essentials with a minimum of tools and experience, and could easily reflect the rider's personality through customized paint jobs and an array of bolt-on parts.

It was within this motorcycle subculture that a more focused outlaw subculture took shape in the 1940s and '50s. Early outlaw motorcycle clubs emphasized mechanical skills and riding ability. Clubs and club members also valued toughness, excitement, and autonomy; the objective of intentionally seeking out trouble was to demonstrate hyper-masculine toughness.

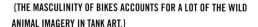

Good Cops, Better Bikes

The outlaw status of motorcycles is impossible to deny. Fifty years of cinema and three generations of bikers have grown up thinking that bikers are bad men and women. Walk into a dealership and it's easy to see the "bad guy" influence through the sheer amount of leather goods available for retail.

However, motorcycles and choppers have also been influenced by the mainstream side of the fence. The most obvious modification borrowed from the law officer is the bore kit. Police vehicles are often modified for higher performance, and the bore kit makes an engine run as if it were bigger. Boring out the cylinder used by the engine and making it bigger compresses more air into the engine. More air means more oxygen for the fuel to react with, and more reaction means more power. While any gearhead worth his wrench can do it on his own, the chopper part companies realized they could simplify the process by selling the kits to the general public.

Another modification was born of the rigors of law enforcement riding. Police riders on long road trips sat in the same position for hours, which was very uncomfortable, as the riding position required being seated with knees bent. Policemen soon discovered that setting the front foot pegs out front and riding in a straight-leg position was more comfortable. Chopper builders began to incorporate this modification, and also to play with the notion of setting the pegs wider apart. If there was ever any question about the sexual metaphor of the motorcy-

{SADDLE BAG, SISSYBAR AND KING-AND-QUEEN SEAT.}

cle, this change answered it with a roaring exclamation.

Riding leathers were adapted from a larger source of law and order. A lot of early bobbers and outlaws like the Booze-fighters and Hell's Angels met each other in the military. While many soldiers found their way into police work after mustering out, a number chafed against the rules and regulations of the military. They also found it difficult to return to a life of suits and manicured lawns, so they picked up a bike and decided to make their own fortune. The first biker jackets were surplus bomber and airman jackets. Some members kept their personal jackets when they left the service. Many of the jackets were further personalized after being on the road for a while: leather

vests were cut from these very well-worn and personally modified jackets.

Airmen also made their bikes into personal statements. Bobbing a bike for performance wasn't enough. The tradition of painting nose art on a plane, which stemmed from naming sea ships and carving intricate mastheads on the bows of wooden sailing ships, continued with tank art. Bobbed bikes no longer resembled the machines the manufacturer envisioned, so why keep its name on the side of the gas tank? Some bobbers just covered the whole bike in a flat matte paint and were done with it. This, too, was a throwback to the military, as many riders came home from the war having learned to ride on a drab military model. Many of these surplus models fell into mechanics' hands and became either fountains of spare parts or side projects. But some bikers painted their own tank art on the side. The art became more and more intricate until having a bike with either a company logo or an original painting became the rule rather than the exception.

Many biker-artists painted war-related emblems on their bikes, and these emblems became symbols of the culture. Allied pilots often used the Maltese cross and the swastika to note how many enemy planes they had downed. When these pilots returned homes and picked up a bike, they already had practice painting these symbols. They

They had risked their lives for the freedom to do what they wanted, so if they wanted to claim their kills on their bike, then so be it.

had risked their lives for the freedom to do what they wanted, so if they wanted to claim their kills on their bike, then so be it. Some riders also used other surplus materials, such as green jackets, helmets, and duty souvenirs. As time wore on and outlaw bikers became the scourge of the highway, the media picked up on the more inflammatory symbols and used them to sensationalize the radical nature of chopper riders. Chances are, a very small number of chopper riders actually wore one of those Kaiser helmets with the spike on top. But Hollywood adapted these symbols easily since movie sets had a lot of spare equipment from old war films.

The chopper and the police bike are forever linked by history and in the American imagination. When people hear the word *motorcycle*, one of these two images pops into the brain. The police bike's most obvious influence is on the modern touring motorcycle. Police bikes were the first to mount large farings on the front and compartments on the back for storage. The chopper has also influenced the look of modern bikes, from the low-riding seat to the iron cross mirrors available at your local dealership. While they may seem to be on opposite sides of the law, both types of bikes are important parts of the modern motorcycle family tree.

The Revolution in Miniature

Choppers were having an effect on American pop culture in many ways by 1965. In addition to the birth of the parts companies and the outlaw biker subgenre of films, an influence on the youth of America was coming that many adults probably missed. Like many great ideas, it started out in the ashes of another grand money-making plan and grew into its own.

Bicycle manufacturer Pearsons Majestic came up with a new seat design. It was long and thin, and the back end of the seat had to be supported by struts bolted onto the wheel. This strange-looking seat originally was meant for the new sport of bicycle polo. The thin seat allowed for better positioning with the mallet and more comfort as the game wore on. While the popularity of polo is unbeatable among British royalty, it didn't catch on with American kids. Pearsons was stuck with its inventory of the strange seats and didn't know where to turn. Luckily, the banana seat of bicycle polo resembled the stretched two-seater choppers that were cropping up in Southern California. The combination of a banana seat and a playing card in the spokes allowed kids a chance to pretend that they were Brando or some other outlaw. Some rumors attribute the first "chopper lite" to the Huffy Corporation, but the forerunner of the chopper bicycle sprung from the mind of Al Fritz, a designer for Schwinn, one of the largest manufacturers of bikes in the world at the time. Coming back from a trip to California, he noticed not only the popularity of choppers but also the modifications that the local kids had made to their own bikes. He took a chance and built a 20-inch bike that borrowed two major design concepts from the choppers of the time. His bike had an elongated seat and a set of ape hanger handlebars that peeled high and away from the low frame of the bicycle. When he showed his designs to his bosses, they balked at first. They didn't like the designs' connotation, but he knew that connotation was precisely the thing that would sell the bike. The Stingray was finally released in June of 1963 and sales took off. The Stingray was the first step in changing the face of bicycles forever. Its high seat and V-shaped handle-

bars are immediately recognizable to anyone who was a child during the era. Even hidden under the white wicker baskets and plastic streamers on the handles, the Stingray was fertile ground for the seeds of the next generation of chopper builders.

Like any innovative idea, the Stingray was soon chased by imitators. The British Raleigh company had used Schwinn designs for years. While their bikes initially didn't make much of a splash, they set themselves apart with the release of the Krate. The Krate took the ideas of the Stingray and added more elements from the chopper subculture. It had different wheel sizes and fender sizes and understood the appeal of a unique-looking bike. Raleigh was happy with it, but wanted its next bike to look

{KIDS SEEING BIKES LIKE THIS HELPED MAKE THE STINGRAY A SUCCESS.}

BIKER SYMBOLISM

The Iron Cross

One of the most common images in the chopper world is the iron cross. The short, squat symbol has been adapted by many chopper houses as the unofficial logo of choppers. Builders needed a distinguishing mark to compete with the distinct bar and shield of Harley-Davidson, so many of them took this symbol from the chopper's past and painted it wherever there was room. The cross, in several variations, is the most widely used religious symbol in military decoration.

The iron cross symbolizes bikers as clearly as the skull and crossbones symbolize pirates. However, the cross has multiple meanings, each one a unique interpretation of the symbols. Nazi Germany tainted the iron cross, but before Hitler, it had been a glorious medal that represented leadership, bravery, and heroism.

The Maltese Cross

The blue or black iron cross is often confused with the red Maltese cross. The significant difference between the two ornaments is in their meaning and place in history. A Maltese cross is made from four straight-lined pointed arrowheads, meeting at their points, with the end of each arm indented in a V. Used as an insignia on the habit of the Knights of Malta, the Maltese cross distinguished them from their enemies. The Knights of Malta, also known as the Knights of St. John or the "Hospitalers," was a religious order founded by Maldivian merchants around the year 1070 to aid and care for pilgrims making the journey to the Holy Land. In 1136, the knights became a fully militarized order. But Islamic forces acquired Malta from Charles V of Spain in 1530 and persecuted the Knights. The Maltese cross evolved into its present-day form as a white, eight-pointed cross. The eight points of the cross represent eight vows: live in truth, have faith, repent of sins, give proof of humility, love justice, be merciful, be sincere and whole-hearted, and endure persecution.

Many countries and organizations use crosses similar to the Maltese cross, but the Maltese cross has a specific meaning and should not be confused with other decorations or medals.

The Skull

It's common to see gruesome skull patches, pins, and tattoos on riders, as well as skull hardware, paint jobs, and sculpture on motorcycles, especially big V-Twin riders and motorcycles. How does the skull fit into the chopper myth, and what has it represented to civilizations past and present?

Skull drawings date back tens of thousands of years and have been found on every continent. They have generally been symbols of mystery, mortality, power, and sometimes evil. Artistically, the skull is a striking symbol that catches the eye and demands attention.

Many believe that the skull is symbolic of wisdom and retained knowledge, as well as physical death (the dying of the flesh) or psychological death (the dying of the self). In old pagan religions, the skull with crossbones stood for the God. The crossed bones beneath the skull symbolized the Slain God and his resurrection from death. In witchcraft, the skull displayed on the front of the cauldron symbolizes renewal through the transformational powers connected with the cauldron. When associated with magic and mysticism, the skull serves as a link to spirits of the Underworld by its association with death.

Probably the skull art that people are most familiar with is by pirates. Seafaring villains like Blackbeard, John Rackham, and Henry Avery used the skull on their flags. Avery's flag displayed a skeletal devil stabbing a human heart. Pirates used skulls and skeletons for their psychological value. A scared individual faced with the possibility of his own death is more easily manipulated than one who's thinking about merely losing money.

Just as effective as the pirate skull was the Nazi skull insignia in WWII, which instilled fear in the hearts of conquered civilians. The real brutality behind the uniform was emphasized by the death's-head symbols.

The use of skulls by soldiers dates back to ancient times, when warriors collected the skulls of their enemies and displayed them as trophies. At times, during WWII for example, even the *good* guys made use of skulls; however, they usually came with the promise of death. A fascinating array of aircraft insignia used in WWII includes the skull along with Disney characters and pin-up girls. The famous winged "Deathshead" of the Hells Angels was developed from the military aircraft insignia of World War II. Since most of the first American bikers were soldiers returning home from war, they were familiar with the icon and used it in their newfound passion.

In the 1960s and early 1970s, a skull pinned on a jacket guaranteed attention. It was a symbol of independence and disdain for the "system." The Grateful Dead and other rock bands adopted skulls and used them on album art, and many T-shirts sported a skull plastered over a marijuana leaf. Even the peaceful, flower-wearing hippies were into the macabre symbol because it was rebellious and cool.

By the late '70s and early '80s, wearing skulls or painting them on a bike had lost some of its appeal, but surprisingly enough, skulls dominate motorcycle art today more than ever before.

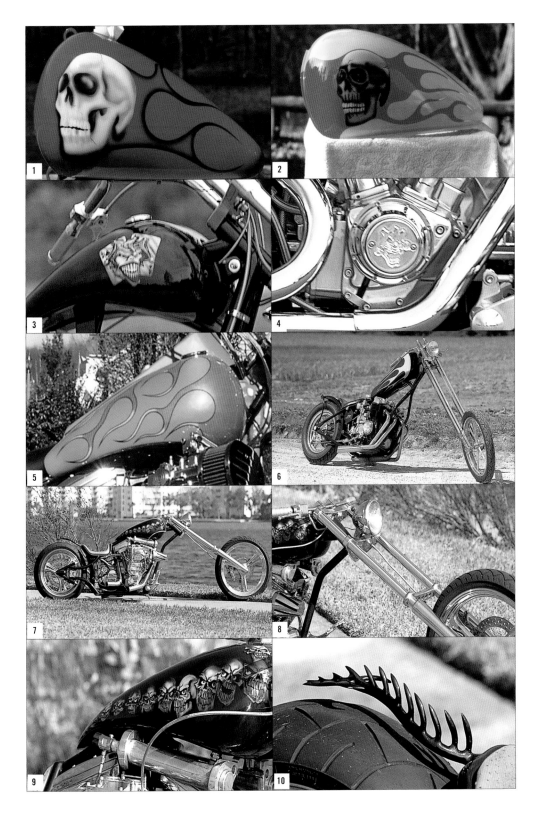

1. {SKULLS HAVE BEEN USED THROUGHOUT HISTORY TO SCARE TRAVELERS INTO SUBMISSION.}
2. {PIRATES USED THE SYMBOL TO GET A MESSAGE ACROSS: "JUST GIVE US YOUR CARGO AND NOBODY WILL GET HURT."}
3. {MANY BIKES SPORT GAMBLING SYMBOLS, LIKE THE JOKER OR THE ACE OF SPADES.}
4. {A POPULAR CARD HAND ON GAS TANKS IS THE DEAD MAN'S HAND—A PAIR OF ACES AND A PAIR OF EIGHTS. IT'S CALLED SUCH BECAUSE WILD BILL HICKOK WAS REPORTED TO BE HOLDING IT WHEN HE WAS SHOT IN THE BACK IN DEADWOOD.}
5. {ANOTHER POPULAR SYMBOL IS THE FLAMES ON THE GAS TANKS.}
6. {POWER FOR FOUR. ROOM FOR ONE.}
7. {THIS BIKE GOES NOT JUST FOR THE SKULL BUT FOR THE SKELETON.}
8. {THE SKULLS START ON THE FRONT . . .}
9. {. . . TRAIL DOWN THE TANK . . .}
10. {. . . AND END AT A SPINE-LIKE BONE STICKING OUT OF THE BACK.}

The combination of a banana seat and a playing card in the spokes allowed kids a chance to pretend that they were Brando or some other outlaw.

even more radical. This bike legitimized the term *chopper*.

The Raleigh Chopper, released in September 1968, took even more design ideas from its bigger brothers. It had a pleated seat with chrome bars that snaked up the rider's back. It allowed pedaling from a low-seated position. The brakes were redesigned to make the bikes look like they had raw open disc brakes. But these modifications also made the bike quite unsafe and unreliable. Kids who rode Raleigh Choppers learned an early lesson about the dangers of their motor-driven brothers. Legislators changed traffic laws in an effort to squeeze choppers off the road; with a similar goal, toy safety advocates pressured bicycle companies to warn parents of the hazards of chopper-style bicycles. A few crusaders even objected on the moral grounds that the banana seat could enable a boy and a girl

to sit on the same bicycle seat. Even though children had ridden two to a bike on the handlebars for years, the outcry concerning the safety of these bikes led to one of the sillier warnings ever levied on a consumer product: the safety strap on the banana seat, which was for the use of a passenger, warned that the seat was meant for only one person.

The heyday of the chopper bike peaked with the golden age of the motorcycle. As motorcycling's popularity declined, kids looked elsewhere for heroes to emulate. Chopper-style bikes were popular throughout most of the 1970s, but then kids started to opt for the all-terrain BMX bike. Chopper bikes were relegated to the yard sales and storage sheds of America until recently. With the resurgence of choppers on the highway, it was only a matter of time until the return of the kid-powered version. In

{YOU'D NEED SOME PRETTY BIG CARDS IN THE SPOKES TO BE HEARD OVER THIS ENGINE.}

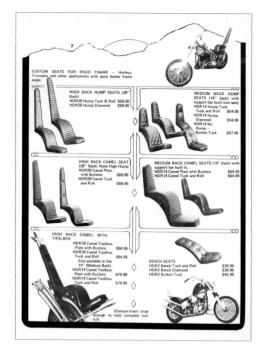

2004, Schwinn released an updated version of the Stingray. Not only did it update the look to bring it in line with the sleeker look of modern choppers, it offered a variety of accessories for customizing the bike. Schwinn Stingray owners can now have bikes with iron cross mirrors and custom seats. In addition, many stores also sell Pocket Rockets, small bikes built with a chopper-style frame and a small gasoline engine. While these bikes are meant for adults, they are just another example of the yearning Americans have to feel like an outlaw chopper biker . . . even if they're only pretending.

The Man Comes Around

At the height of the initial surge of chopper popularity, forces moved in to hinder the builders from pushing their art's boundaries. At the start of the phenomenon, if a few crazy custom guys decided to take their lives into their own hands, it didn't really matter. But as custom bikes became a business and more of them made their way onto the highway, people took notice of them not just for their unique styling, but also for the dangers the modifications posed. Chopper riders were living fast and dying young, and the corpses they were leaving weren't very beautiful.

A lot of the modifications being made affected the motorcycles themselves. Traffic cops saw the lack of front brakes as a safety hazard. Those low frames scraped against the ground as they rode along America's bumpy highways. And nothing put cage drivers on edge like a half dozen choppers roaring down the highway.

The first legal crackdown was a flurry of hotly contested helmet laws. Many chopper riders violated the laws flagrantly. After all, if the bike isn't street legal, the rider's lack of head protection seems to be a side issue. Motorcycle manufacturers quietly endorsed

the laws and came out on the side of the police. While many riders believed helmets interfered with the riding experience, many others saw it as a message to those undesirable chopper riders: if you're crazy enough to take your life into your own hands by riding a hand-built bike, you should also take responsibility for wearing a helmet.

Ironically, by the time safety crackdowns started to take effect, the choppers being built were safer. Aftermarket companies like AEE were manufacturing standardized accessories that were made of the proper materials and tested for proper use. Kit-bashing spare parts made for other bikes meant that bolt holes didn't always line up and bikes were twisted in ways that the guys with engineering degrees couldn't imagine. But parts made in actual machine shops fit better and made better bikes.

European Competition

Because of increased competition from other modes of transportation in the 1950s, rider-

{NOTE THE CAPTAIN AMERICA–STYLE HELMET IN THE CORNER.}

Chopper riders were living fast and dying young, and the corpses they were leaving weren't very beautiful.

ship was being whittled down to a hard core of riders who truly enjoyed the sensation and rigor that only motorcycles can provide. Technical skill and mechanical knowledge were still important but not essential; potential buyers needed transportation that was reliable and versatile. In the U.S., the best bikes barely survived, and after World War I, they provided cheap and utilitarian transportation. Despite technical advances that improved speed, handling, and comfort, the domestic market for motorcycles became increasingly narrow.

Motorcycles fared better in Europe, possibly because of the industry's infrastructure and less intense competition from automobile companies. In America, the Harley-Davidson Motorcycle Company stressed service from the beginning. Its efforts to establish a national network of dealers and parts suppliers, along with

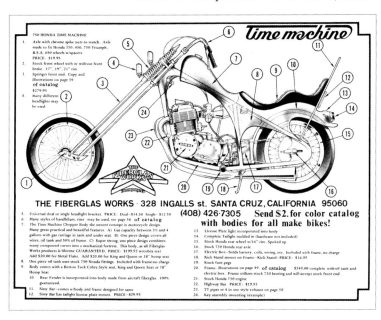

{COMPANIES BEGAN TO SELL PARTS THAT COULD BE ATTACHED TO A VARIETY OF BIKES.}

its intrinsic conservatism, may have kept the company afloat during the lean years between wars. European firms also had the advantage of years of experience, and could take advantage of geographical and climatic differences. To survive, Harley-Davidson pitched its line of reliable, heavy-duty bikes to its two prime markets: police departments and the military. The Department of the Interior used Harleys to patrol Yellowstone National Park, and delivery drivers and rural letter carriers went about their jobs on Servi-cars and sidecar-equipped motorbikes.

European manufacturers, especially those in Great Britain and Germany, dominated the youthful motorcycle market in the '60s. Industry histories concentrate on European designs and innovations; Harley-Davidson, Indian, and other American makes rate only brief asides. The explanation for this focus is fairly simple: the look of a motorcycle is as important as manufacturing and sales. Even slight changes in design, like the placement of the gearshift or the location of the speedometer, become major issues. Dealers concentrated almost exclu-

{THIS SPRINGER HARDTAIL IS NOT A COMFORTABLE LONG-DISTANCE RIDE.}

sively on European bikes, and many experts offered European machines as "yardsticks" of motorcycle engineering.

Styling was not an immediate concern in this country, however. Size and power mattered most. After introducing a V-twin (two cylinders mounted in a V shape) in 1909, Harley-Davidson dominated the American market. Big bikes, twins, and fours (four cylinders), came to define this country's motorcycles. And despite flirtation with smaller bikes and fours, Harley-Davidson's conservative focus on large-displacement twins (750–1,400 cc's) earned it a reputation for intractability and stagnation. German and British firms concentrated on speed and handling, and on perfecting their small-bore single- and twin-cylinder engines.

To Europeans, stodgy Harleys and Indians were huge and unwieldy. Only in America did the styling of hogs and Super Chiefs come to be considered classic. But the obvious reason for this focus on size was the need for motorcycles to compare to automobiles in terms of comfort and tank size. American motorcycles had to travel farther between fuel stops than smaller European models. If American manufacturers needed a rationale for big bikes, that was it. But inherent design limitations hurt the motorcycle's American marketability. It could not comfortably transport a family (unless the rider had a sidecar). Also, it was at the mercy of weather. Early

on, cars had similar problems and "automobilists" stored their vehicles in the winter, but by 1914 some cars had roll-up windows and heaters, and the Fisher Closed Body Corporation turned out 150 enclosed chassis in 1910. Henry Ford's Dearborn, Michigan, assembly line hit its stride in the 1920s, churning out cars that for $245 compared favorably to the cost of a two-wheeler. In the end, most Americans turned their backs on bikes. Harley-Davidson's production of motorcycles dropped by almost two-thirds—28,189 to 10,202—from 1920 to 1921, and it would not top that 1920 sales figure again until 1942.

Motorcycling's image was further damaged by the deaths of a number of high-profile racers in the 1920s. Motordromes, which were often just steeply banked wooden tracks, were regularly referred to as "murderdromes." By the 1930s, flat-track and dirt-track racing had lost their luster, and road construction and the automobile made cross-country runs less than appealing. Outside of delivery drivers and police officers, motorcycling became the province of the eccentric and the antisocial. Harley-Davidson, always a wizard at advertising and public relations, began to stress respectability and recreational themes in pitching its product. The company used its in-house publication, *The Enthusiast*, to promote safe riding. It was, and still is, "a publication that cultivates and celebrates much of what is good about riding in the company of like-minded people."

BENNETT'S FOLLY

1. {THE ENGINE IS A CLASSIC HARLEY KNUCKLEHEAD.}
2. {THE KICK-START IS A CLASSIC FEATURE OF CHOPPERS THAT IS NOT SEEN ON MANY MODERN BIKES.}

A cross-country endurance ride by Wells Bennett in 1922 illustrates many of the hazards faced by this country's early bikers. Riding a Henderson four, Bennett left Los Angeles and within fifty miles ran out of paved road. From there on, one-third of his route was composed of sand and gravel cut with deep ruts. Plugging along to Flagstaff, Arizona, in second gear mile after mile, Bennett had trouble keeping his balance. He had to cross from one side of the road to the other many times to keep in the furrows. This was very strenuous. After Flagstaff, he came to the mountains and bounced over sixty-eight miles of assorted rocks, chuck holes, and sand, only occasionally getting out of low gear.

Outside of Winslow, Arizona, Wells fell into a dry wash and his 450-pound bike sank into the sand. The trip continued in a similar vein, with the occasional sand dune thrown in for variety, until he hit Emporia, Kansas, after one hundred hours in the saddle. From St. Louis to New York City he had the advantage of paved roads, but cold October nights wearied him, and a brush with streetcar rails left him bruised and battered on the side of a New Jersey highway. He managed to set a transcontinental speed record—six days, fifteen hours and thirteen minutes—an improvement of some seven hours over the previous mark, but only because the weather had been dry and his bike suffered no damage more serious than a series of flat tires.

Before World War I, attempting a lengthy trip on a small bike with a limited fuel capacity was folly. In the 1920s and '30s, a cyclist could hope for, at best, five thousand miles before having to discard an off-brand bike; American-made motorcycles were not mechanically sound. The dependability offered by Harley-Davidson and Indian became increasingly important, as did the dealer's mechanical support. Aside from mechanical innovation, in the United States the automobile quickly displaced the motorcycle as a symbol of middle-class striving. A car in the garage (or more likely on the curb) was a sure sign of success. The motorcycle's working-class image has never been completely overcome.

[THE DETAIL ON THIS HAND-PAINTED TANK IS AMAZING.]

Contradiction in Terms

The late 1970s signified the death of the chopper to many. Until the resurgence of the past few years, choppers had been relegated to the annals of motor vehicle history, rarely seen outside of old movies and auto shows. The '70s were lean years for many people and the motorcycle industry was hit hard. Motorcycles had long since moved out of the category of necessary transportation and become a hobbyist's vehicle, like a boat or a second car. Justifying such an expense was difficult. The influx of cheaper, more powerful motorcycles from Japan and abroad put American motorcycle manufacturers in dire straits. In desperation, the motorcycle industry made a move into chopper territory with a bike called the "factory custom."

The factory custom is closely married to the cruiser-style motorcycle. The cruiser took a lot of style cues from the chopper. It had raised handlebars as well as a lowered seat. It had an ever-so-slightly extended front end and looked just enough like a chopper for the public to make the connection subconsciously. It was the middle ground between the big long-distance bikes and the smaller, sportier models. The factory custom idea made customizing the cruiser as easy as turning a few bolts and riding down to the local dealership for parts.

After years of denying the connection between choppers and mainstream bikes, the manufacturers were doing the unthinkable: they were embracing the outlaw image and touting it in their ads and on their sleeves. While initial attempts were unsuccessful, the idea eventually caught on, and now the concept is one of the backbones of the industry. The factory custom idea defines the look and feel of today's motorcycle.

The aftermarket accessory companies had the right idea and the manufacturers exploited it. You can choose the accessories on a new car, but beyond that the vehicle's appearance is set. Motorcycles, on the other hand, have hundreds of small parts that can be switched out—handlebars, rear-view mirrors, gas caps, and so on. By changing each of these parts, the rider makes the bike unique. Such parts are relatively easy to remove and install

{THE EXTENDED FORK OFFERS A LEANER LOOK AT A HIGHER TURN RADIUS.}

{THIS CRUISER LOOK IS OFTEN CONFUSED FOR A "FACTORY CUSTOM."}

{YOU CAN BUY SEATS JUST LIKE THIS AS A BOLT-ON ACCESSORY.}

at a dealership. Also, this off-the-rack customization keeps customers coming back for voluntary maintenance—a rider can update the look of his bike by replacing his current parts with trendy new ones. Factory customs provide all the fun of a chopper without the risk or hard work.

Many builders scoff at the idea—it's the difference between paint-by-numbers and a blank canvas. But the idea drew in a new customer base as kids growing up riding those Stingrays took their first baby steps into the world of custom bike building. The idea helped keep motorcycles alive until the industry's upswing in the 1980s and '90s.

By keeping motorcycling alive, the manufacturers kept choppers alive as well. While not directly accepting them, they began to adapt to the images long associated with motorcycles. Clubs were less about formal attire and family fun and more about having fun and riding around the world. Dealerships opened themselves up to other types of bikes and some opened up their own custom shops on the side. The custom community, proud of its outlaw image, also had to deal with the change in social norms. More and more people were coming into the sport and embracing the ideas that long-time builders had been using for years. It became more difficult to tell the difference between a real rider and someone who played dress-up on

{BUT NOTHING BEATS THE LOOK OF A TRUE CHOPPER.}

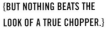

{THE SLIM TANK OFFERS LESS MILEAGE BUT MORE SEXINESS.}

the weekends. Many long-term riders didn't care about the difference between riders and welcomed the influx. The sport received a lot of fresh bodies from the Vietnam War, many of them signing on for the same reasons their forerunners in the 1950s and '60s had done.

The factory custom concept bridged the gap between custom eras. Until the third generation of custom bike builders came into their own, factory custom provided a stopgap that satisfied both sides of the sport. Neither side could anticipate what was in store, as both the factory custom and the chopper would soon evolve from counterculture icon to affluent status symbol.

The 1980s Strike Back

For most of the 1980s, motorcycles operated under the pop culture radar. Thirty years after Hollister and twenty years after *Easy Rider*, they existed in the lawless fringes of the imagination. Like many pop culture villains, bikers lost their credibility as bad guys. A few films, such as *Streets of Fire,* tried to recapture the spark of *The Wild One*

but got only the music right. While Tom Cruise's hot-shot pilot rode a motorcycle on the ground in *Top Gun*, the real ride everybody wanted was his F-14 Tomcat.

The manufacturers were embroiled in their own war. A flood of Japanese import bikes hit the market and caught Harley-Davidson just as it was coming out of a troubled era. It had finally pulled away from American Machine and Foundry and was struggling to find its place in a slim market. The conflict between American pride in its industry and the American need for bargains was being fought on many fronts, and the automotive industry battle was one of the ugliest of this war. Drivers were put off during the oil crisis of the late 1970s and sought economical imports.

Honda debuted the new Goldwing in 1980. This bike was a departure from the previous model years and was an open challenge to the touring bikes that were sustaining Harley-Davidson. The Goldwing appealed to bikers who wanted the same feel as a touring bike but weren't willing to pay homegrown prices.

Harley struck back with an aggressive pricing war. It made an unprecedented offer: buy a Sportster, hang onto it for a year, and use its trade-in value toward the price of another bike. Some say it was a brilliant move, others claim it was born out of desperation, and still others suggest the company had a surplus of Sportsters that it wanted to get rid of. Regardless of the company's motives, more Americans than ever before bought Harleys as the Baby Boomers were coming of age.

Rich Urban Bikers

Thanks to the renaissance of motorcycles, choppers are in the public eye again. With all the TV shows and increased public awareness, bikes and bikers have finally moved into mainstream America. One of the most profitable companies in America these days is Harley-Davidson. Riding is a popular and increasingly acceptable way to spend a weekend (or a paycheck.) Events like charity rides make good public relations, and nowadays you really can meet the nicest people on a Harley-Davidson. It provides the ultimate weekend getaway—with the wind in the hair and the flapping fringe of leather chaps on Sunday—for all those parents and coworkers who are so responsible and buttoned down during the week.

All this seems to fly in the face of the rebel culture that used to be associated with motorcycles, and especially Harleys. The motorcycle lifestyle is rapidly becoming an image that can be purchased, almost like buying a membership to a country club. These image-conscious riders have been termed "RUBs" or Rich Urban Bikers. The growing popularity and social acceptance of motorcycling is being fueled by its mainstream participants. They might be trying to buy an antisocial image, but the most antisocial thing they are likely to do is mount some loud pipes on that hog.

Thirty years after Hollister and twenty years after *Easy Rider*, they existed in the lawless fringes of the imagination.

{THE EVOLUTION ENGINE IS THE HEART OF THIS BIKE.}

While cars are a necessity, choppers are a dream. They are clouds and thunder pulled from the sky and wrapped in steel and chrome.

The motorcycle industry has changed a lot in the last fifteen years. When many bikers started riding in the 1960s, the wrong kind of crowd rode Harley-Davidsons. The feeling was that the good people rode something else. Many motels and campgrounds didn't allow motorcyclists. Today, campgrounds welcome bikers and organized bike tours are everywhere. Motorcycling has caught up with the times.

Many bikers note with a hint of nostalgia that the lifestyle has become commercialized, has emerged as a commodity to be packaged, bought and sold. Some old-school bikers understand how the old mountain men felt as they saw civilization march westward. While it is nice to have more people to talk to, such widespread acceptance of motorcycles is forcing the subculture to conform to the wishes of the majority.

So the next time you see an individual who still lives the old biker ways, admire how the guy still builds his own ride and still talks of brotherhood. He's part of a vanishing breed that still believes in the individuality and rebellion that created the biker culture. He still remembers what it used to be about.

The Future of Choppers

Almost forty years have passed since the birth of the chopper, born out of the DNA of bobbers, LSD, and hot California summers. The chopper has become a symbol of personal freedom, sexual liberation, unbridled expression, and a dangerous lifestyle. From its humble beginnings as a backyard hobby through its rise, fall, and resurrection, the chopper has grabbed the American psyche in a way few other vehicles have. While cars are a necessity, choppers are a dream. They are clouds and thunder pulled from the sky and wrapped in steel and chrome.

Most experts believe the current boom of motorcycle awareness won't last past the next few years. People tune in to the popular TV show *American Chopper* more to see the Tuttles fight than to see the bike. What goes up must come down, and just as it has before, America will leave its love affair

with motorcycles for a while. The second generation of choppers will be packed away in collective nostalgia. People will move onto the next fad and the die-hards will once again reassert themselves.

But the idea of the rolling sculpture that is the motorcycle will never die. In those backwoods and burned-out places, someone will get the bright idea to change his stock bike and push the envelope again. While the celebrity rub might not return, it will draw them like moths to the flame. Just like the wheels it rides on, the chopper will roll back again—bigger, meaner, and nastier than before.

ROAD OUTLAWS
AND ORGANIZATIONS

{LONG HAIR AND HIGH BARS ARE THE EASIEST WAYS FOR THE
STRAIGHTS TO SPOT THE OUTLAWS.}

{The biker is one of the most American characters ever created.}

The motorcycle outlaw is one of the strongest pop culture symbols of the twentieth century. In many ways, the biker is one of the most American characters ever created—the modern cowboy with his own rules, an ability to wander wherever he likes, and a wolf mentality are part of the allure of the outlaw. Whether the image made the man or the man made the image is debatable. But the organizations like the Hell's Angels are all very real.

Bobbers, Choppers, and Outlaws

Most members of post–WWII outlaw clubs were unskilled or semi-skilled laborers. They escaped otherwise dull lives through the excitement generated by the club. The motorcycle provided mechanically inclined, working-class youths a level playing field on which to compete in those skills that were important to them. They suspended competition in a game they could not win—middle-class striving—by creating and emphasizing an artificial culture in which they made their own rules.

In the years immediately following World War II, the AMA recognized that riders and clubs were gaining media attention for their ill-mannered behavior, but it believed they represented only one percent of all motorcyclists. Clubs that did not abide by AMA bylaws became, by definition, outlaws.

Exactly who comprised the original outlaw clubs remains something of a mystery. In his book *Hell's Angels: A Strange & Terrible Saga of the Outlaw Motorcycle Gang*, Hunter Thompson argues that the Southern California chapters were the offspring of "Okies" and "Arkies" who fled the Dust Bowl during the Depression. Harley historian Martin Norris and others believe they were air force veterans who stepped off troop trains in California and decided to stay. That Harley-Davidson produced about ninety thousand motorcycles during World War II and then trained servicemen to ride and repair them supports the contention that veterans familiar with Harleys would continue to ride them upon return to civilian life. Why they would take up a vagabond and sometimes outlaw lifestyle is another question.

One publication states the clubs were composed of veterans who could not adjust to the boredom of civilian life or who simply rejected the idea to prewar patterns. Since they were still few in number, they tended to band together. California provided perfect weather as well as a developing interstate highway system ideal for motorcycle riding. In the 1950s, motorcycling and the culture surrounding it meant excitement as well as a sense of camaraderie. The West Coast became a mecca for gangs of ten to thirty young men on powerful machines who roamed the highways in search of adventure, and when none could be found they created their own.

Outlaw clubs were difficult to ignore as they took to disrupting AMA-sanctioned events. *Life* magazine and Hollister, California, provided the country its initial image of these clubs in 1947. The July Fourth Hollister hill climb and races also provided the turning point for motorcycling in America, forever damaging the image of all bikers. As mentioned in

{THIS BIKE LOOKS SHARP . . .}

{... IN MANY SENSES OF THE WORD.}

California, (1964); and Weirs Beach, New Hampshire, (1965).

A famous (or infamous) Hollister photograph from *Life* magazine features a bike parked with its front wheel spoke deep in a pile of beer bottles. The rider on the bike looks sweaty, fat, and surly, and he is clutching a pair of bottles in his hands. The biker seems ready to let out a belch so horrific that the smell will reach the viewer of the picture. This picture haunted many folks in their dreams. They had heard the stories of unruly motorcyclists tearing up towns and making off with virtuous daughters, but here was the vivid image of a glassy-eyed, boozing, hell-raising, leather-wearing biker. How long, people wondered, till this barbarian would tear through their neighborhood, leaving the quiet streets looking like a war zone?

{EVEN THE WHEELS LOOK DEADLY.}

chapter 1, reports of attendance vacillate from 1,500 to as many as 3,000 cyclists. In addition to the riding events, the weekend also included drinking, carousing, and cycle hooliganism. Some of the riders were arrested at some point during the weekend—probably Friday night—but they were freed by another mob of riders who broke into the jail Saturday. AMA officials insisted that many of the motorized groups that had converged on the town were not sanctioned by the association, and the mayhem had been committed by those unsanctioned groups.

After the chaos at Hollister, mainstream media reported similar disturbances at other events. Over the next twenty years, violent incidents transpired in Angels Camp, California, (1957); Porterville, California, (1963); Laconia, New Hampshire, and Monterey,

There was one problem: the photograph was taken weeks after the rally, the bike was borrowed from a local, and the photograph was anything but legitimate. After reading accounts of that July Fourth weekend in the *San Francisco Chronicle*, *Life* magazine dispatched reporters to Hollister. Wanting a photo to go along with their two-paragraph article, reporters swept as many bottles as they could find into a pile, borrowed Don Middleton's motorcycle, and asked if he would be willing to pose, beer bottles in hand, for a few pictures. Gus Depersa, a lifetime Hollister resident, says he witnessed the whole ordeal. He claims to be the gentleman in the background of the posed picture.

The immediate result for bikers was increased police scrutiny of motorcycle club activities—legal and illegal alike.

Hollister divided bikers into separate camps. One side doted on full-dress touring bikes and presenting a positive image, while the other side—the Hollister rowdies—rode bikes in various stages of modification, ready to perform violent or outrageous behavior. The bikers who disrupted Hollister were probably members of recognized clubs, either POBOBs (Pissed Off Bastards of Bloomington) or Boozefighters. These clubs, along with the Market Street Commandoes and the Galloping Gooses, provided the foundation for the Hell's Angels.

Hell's Angels

Though the Hell's Angels constitute just one of many outlaw clubs, their place in the subculture must be considered separately. Society was introduced to the club by William Murray's 1965 *Saturday Evening Post* article. Without a lot of bluster, he described the Angel lifestyle and philosophy and explained the various outlaw symbols (pins, badges, tattoos, and Nazi paraphernalia), focusing on the Angels' interest in shocking "squares" and "citizens" in order to gain and maintain their freedom. While he concluded they were unpredictable and dangerous as a group, Murray's overall picture suggested chronic malcontents that were ultimately harmless. It also described a shallow lifestyle with no identifiable boundaries between moral and immoral—one that a certain segment of society found attractive.

{THIS TANK ALLOWS THE RIDER TO SEE INSIDE.}

(NOT ALL CHOPPERS ARE CRUISERS.)

America couldn't stop talking about the outlaws and their bikes, even though respectable citizens were supposedly repulsed and turned off by them.

Plenty of people were unhappy with the way the world was, so the nomad lifestyle of the outlaw biker and his stretched-out chopper had a definite appeal. By 1965, the first steps had already been taken.

Despite efforts by the AMA and the motorcycle industry to maintain a positive image of two-wheeled life, public fear received another jolt from journalist Hunter Thompson. Thompson did a wonderful job of pointing out that America couldn't stop talking about the outlaws and their bikes, even though respectable citizens supposedly were repulsed and turned off by them. He also recounted how a Hell's Angels run attracted an unreasonable amount of police, media, and public attention. His ironic tone struck at the core of the chopper's image problem. If outlaw bikers didn't want anyone to bother them, why did they draw so much attention to themselves? If the police wanted to end the scourge of choppers, why did they make a big deal about busting chopper riders? Everyone, it seemed, was just playing a role.

That sense of irony changed sometime during his continuing research for *Hell's Angels*, however. His criticism of news reports and police bias against bikers remains in the text, but Thompson also sug-

gests that the media failed to comprehend the danger of its continual hounding of the bikers. Thompson chronicles the sense of difference consciously cultivated by Angels to keep the public at a distance. Through the skillful use of fear and violence, outlaw clubs gained what they truly wanted: to be left alone. By the end of the book, any romantic notions of two-wheeled outlaws had been replaced by the reality that the Hell's Angels were a band of ill-mannered thugs bent on violence and sexual depravity. Thompson was disturbed by such devi-

ance and disconcerted that some elements of society would find the outlaw clubs' brand of violence attractive.

Thompson's association with the Hell's Angels coincided with the release of the California attorney general's report *The Hell's Angels Motorcycle Club*, also known as the Lynch Report. Attorney General Thomas Lynch, acting on the request of State Senator Fred Farr, investigated the activities of outlaw motorcycle clubs operating in California. The request followed the alleged rape of two Monterey girls, ages 14 and 15, by a number of Hell's Angels. Four club members were arrested but the charges were later dropped for lack of evidence. The sixteen-page report made an impressive splash when it was released in 1965. *Time, Newsweek*, and the *New York Times*, as well as many other news organizations, picked up on the report and gave it national prominence—more attention than it deserved, according to some historians.

The Lynch Report did succeed in feeding the media's frenzy to disclose the particulars of biker deviance. Lynch's survey of California's police and sheriff's departments documented eighteen instances that, taken together, were meant to reveal an insidious and threatening cancer growing in the

{THE ORGAN PIPES ARE A GOOD WAY TO DRAW ATTENTION.}

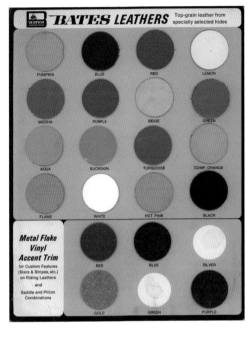

state's poorer neighborhoods. The report offered a short history of outlaw clubs and detailed their interest in drug trafficking, theft, assault, and rape. The incendiary section was titled "Hoodlum Activities." Arrogant outlaw bikers raped, robbed, and pillaged with abandon, it charged, threatening anyone who stood in their way. Few charges were brought against them because their victims were usually too afraid to testify against them. The report had everything a sensational news story should have: sex, violence, criminals, and debauchery.

The final section, "Recommendations by Law Enforcement Officials," suggested response options for law enforcement officials. The most effective action, one police chief noted, was to meet force with force. Officers involved in situations with chopper riders should expect them to draw weapons

and attempt to beat and murder them, the report suggested.

Regarding the inability to find witnesses against the Angels, the document noted that the club exploited the "gangster's code" by requiring fierce loyalty and by intimidating anyone who stood against them. The report also noted, however, that much of the club's terrorism was aimed at those who ran in the same circles as the Hell's Angels as opposed to folks on Main Street. In other words, the club members' violence was aimed at those who, like themselves, were lower class and might be engaged in illegal activities.

In *Hell's Angels* Thompson minimized the content of the report. His strongest criticism was aimed at the *Times* article that reported that members of the club raped the two girls in Monterey but did not acknowledge that the charges had been

BATES Grip-Tite HANDLEBARS

Heavy-gauge steel...triple-chrome plated...twelve popular styles

Bates *Grip-Tite* Handlebars won't slip, even during rugged competition, because they are knurled at all critical points to give positive, non-slip control.

These bars are formed from special heavy-gauge steel tubing for maximum strength...and triple-chrome plated to a gleaming finish. Knurling is on the underside of bars to preserve their beautiful appearance.

Twelve popular styles assure a complete choice for comfort, safety and maneuverability. Diameter is ⅞".

SUPER-LITE ALUMINUM ALLOY HANDLEBARS
One-third the weight of steel...ideal for racing. Luster finish resists corrosion and tarnishing. No knurling is needed or supplied on alloy bars.

KNURLING AT THREE POINTS
Bates puts the knurling where you need it: at the brake and throttle controls, clutch control and fork head mount. Knurling is on the underside only and does not show—yet provides a positive, non-slip control.

16

BATES LUGGAGE RACKS

...the most beautiful racks made for cycles.

Three distinctive rack styles...each one a masterful combination of functional utility and jewel-like chrome plating. Every rack has been designed to mount in minutes with a neat, custom fit. Extra large rack surface...136 square inches of carrying space. Bates special handrails and backrests... plus many other features make these the finest racks available.

Other special features

(1) Concealed rope ties give a quick sure place to hook bungee cords, etc.

(2) Removable "non-slip" holders...help keep books, lunch box, etc., from slipping.

dropped. In summarizing the events that transpired after the release of the attorney general's report, Thompson wrote that the news reports manipulated the rest of the country's media. The Hell's Angels discussed by the media and the Hell's Angels that Thompson researched were two very different animals.

People were outraged at the bikers' brutality, but outlaw clubs survived the attention of law enforcement officials in spite of—or possibly because of—media exposure that kept them in the public eye. Their outrageous behavior made them a regular feature on the local, national and international level. Entertainment media further romanticized the lifestyle and fed outlaw clubs recruits, even when the images were meant to illustrate the evils of biker culture.

In 1971, the Rolling Stones hired the Hell's Angels as security for the Altamont music festival, which was expected to be a second Woodstock. The reality, however, was somewhat different, as documented in the film *Gimme Shelter*. The Hell's Angels took their job seriously. During the concert, a group of Angels stomped and stabbed a young black man who either threatened a gang member with a gun or vandalized their motorcycles, depending on whose story you read. The murder was caught on film, and the

glare of publicity not only helped bring an end to the Age of Aquarius, but further demonized biker culture.

A few years earlier, in 1967, Thompson had noted that the initial incentive for the formation of outlaw clubs had gone. No longer did they band together for brotherhood and the freedom of the open road, or to protect their privacy and a way of life. Instead, they existed simply to uphold the deviant image they had promoted. In the early 1970s, the Angels took over other motorcycle clubs, incorporated, and set their course for the future. Out of necessity they cut their ties to the media and removed themselves as much as possible from the public eye. This, combined with an invasion of high-quality Japanese imports, allowed the motorcycle industry and the AMA to begin a concerted effort to clean up their image and promote cycling as a wholesome hobby and sport for the entire family.

Harley Cleans Up Its Image

After Hollister, Harley-Davidson tried to disassociate itself from outlaw bikers, but it was difficult and maybe detrimental because it was the hard core of Harley enthusiasts and outlaws that kept the company solvent through its most turbulent years. No longer could Harley-Davidson depend on the military or police departments to keep it in business. With the encroachment of Japanese motorcycles beginning in 1959, Harley embarked on a long and arduous climb back to the top.

Honda's early marketing plan was to emphasize what it did best—small-bore motorcycles and scooters—in order to establish a beachhead in America. A new market of young people, especially college students, was attracted to these bikes as cheap and easy transportation. Only later, as their share of the market grew, did Japanese manufacturers challenge Harley-Davidson's superiority in heavyweights and touring bikes. Unfortunately, Harley-Davidson

{THE JAGGED Z-BAR GIVES A BIKE A ROUGHER LOOK.}

ignored the growing influence of Japanese models. Its scramble to develop engines that could match the technologically advanced four-strokes and produce more stylish models came too late. In 1968, to evade a hostile takeover, Harley-Davidson was sold to American Machine & Foundry (AMF) to bolster that company's recreational products line.

AMF, however, made its own mistakes in facing the Japanese challenge. It attempted to change Harley-Davidson's emphasis to lightweights, but despite success on racetracks, Harley faithful would not accept the new bikes, and dealers simply turned their backs and focused only on the hogs of earlier days. AMF added to its problems by increasing production without improving quality control. Consequently, dealers had to service and repair most new bikes before they could even go on the sales floor. Just as AMF began mending its relationship with dealers and motorcyclists, and began development of a new engine design, the company changed its corporate strategy away from recreational products.

A group of Harley-Davidson executives and stockholders bought the company in 1981 and set it on the road to profitability. The new owners began improving the bike's battered image by instituting quality control

{HIGH BARS MEAN A LOW RIDER POSITION.}

{JUST BECAUSE IT'S A SINGLE CYLINDER DOESN'T MEAN IT'S NOT MACHO.}

{THE SNUG SEAT DOESN'T OFFER MUCH SHOCK ABSORPTION.}

measures and assigning ambassadors to regain customer good will. They established HOG (Harley Owners Group) as a means of emphasizing after-sales service. They dealt with the leather and denim image by taking aim at dealers who perpetuated a "bad-guy" image. Harley dealerships, the company felt, were too often located in run-down areas and could not cater to the new family image Harley-Davidson sought. Dealers were told to clean up their acts, to stop treating owners of Japanese motorcycles (hence potential Harley owners) with contempt, and to reach out to new customers through Harley's new product lines and "boutique-quality" clothing.

The Harley-Davidson Motorcycle Company edged into the black in 1983 and by 1986 was confident enough to

{THE CURVED TANK OFFERS MORE ROOM FOR THE ENGINE.}

{THIS HARDTAIL DESIGN IS FOR THE HARDCORE RIDER.}

support the removal of tariffs on Japanese bikes. Once again it was cool to tool around on a Harley and wear a leather jacket. Unfortunately, Harley's success priced even low-end Sportsters out of the reach of the most faithful of enthusiasts.

The company's movement into the mainstream and its emphasis on an expensive line of clothing and fashion accessories alienated those who created, championed, and popularized the image being exploited by Harley-Davidson. The biker image was sanitized in an effort to make it safe for rich urban bikers and wannabe bikers. The Harley-Davidson company of the 1980s and 1990s preferred to accentuate patriotism, freedom, and just a hint of nonconformity rather than emphasize

its outlaw roots. It even attempted to market the outlaw essence of motorcycling through a signature line of cologne.

But America's muddled adoration of deviance, individuality, and masculinity have kept the biker myth alive. Despite a marketing emphasis on utility and economy, the motorcycle continues to attract men with something to prove. Controlling eight hundred pounds of steel balanced on two wheels demands skill, strength and a certain fearlessness, as does opposing anxious and arrogant motorists who begrudge the highway to such intruders. The motorcycle industry successfully minimizes consumers' worries about the potential loss of life and limb by emphasizing the freedom

of riding the open road, the rush of wind in the hair, and the ability to go where one pleases. But such freedom comes at a cost: putting one's life on the line in order to seize a moment of "deviant" pleasure is paying a dear price for masculinity.

One Percenters

The hard-drinking, hard-riding, hard-fisted phenomenon of the Hell's Angels Motorcycle Club was kick-started not on America's highways, but in the world's deadly and bleeding fields of war. The Angels have grown over the past fifty years to include three dozen chapters in the United States, a presence in fifteen countries, and a worldwide membership estimated in the thousands.

But before all that—before roving bands of unwashed malcontents began riding the West astride iron horses like gun-slinging outlaws, before they tore open America's fabric and sewed themselves into the tapestry of mainstream culture, before they bathed and broke out as businessmen, before all that—their name belonged to other Angels.

"Hell's Angels" was a name long favored by mercenaries and soldiers who risked all for principle, belief, freedom, and individual rights, including the right to ride big Harley-Davidson hogs. Many believe the original Angels were members of the U.S. Army's Eleventh Airborne Division, an elite group of paratroopers trained to rain death on the enemy from above after drifting in behind the lines of battle in the Second World War. They called themselves the Hell's Angels because they flew on silk wings into hell itself, bringing a brutal hope of peace with twenty pounds of TNT strapped to each leg. The nickname was a badge of honor, a mark of invincibility, and a wartime emblem indicating the toughest of the tough. It was a totem to ward off the worst.

Not surprisingly, a handful of those original Hell's Angels, along with many other returning soldiers who had lived the nightmare of war, found it difficult to settle into the half-sleep of the American Dream. After having lived on the edge so long, they found only a depressing fatalism and monotony

"Hell's Angels" was a name long favored by mercenaries and soldiers who risked all for principle, belief, freedom, and individual rights, including the right to ride big Harley-Davidson hogs.

{THAT'S NOT JUST A SPIKE—IT'S A GAS CAP.}

in career, family, mortgages, college, suburbia, and cookie-cutter houses with white-picket fences.

So they rode. Motorcycles were cheap in the mid-1940s when sold as military surplus, and they offered a certain wild peacetime freedom not unlike the wartime skies of Europe. Soon, individuals gathered into groups, sharing weekends when they rode hard and partied harder. But when Monday came, not everyone went home. Some stayed, turning the weekend motorcycle club into a surrogate family of full-time brothers.

Two of the first such fraternities were the Pissed Off Bastards and the Boozefighters, early groups that established the notoriety of the outlaw biker image. When they arrived in Hollister, the Pissed Off Bastards rode in drunk, wild, and destructive, landing as if behind enemy lines with a belly full of TNT. The local sheriff later described the scene as "just one hell of a mess."

Quick to control the public relations damage, the AMA denounced the Bastards, saying it was unfortunate that one percent of motorcyclists should ruin everything for the law-abiding ninety-nine percent. To this day, the one-percent insignia remains a badge of honor, worn with pride by those who live outside of that milquetoast ninety-nine percent majority who ride whining Hondas back and forth to the office.

After Hollister, internal tension among the Bastards and Boozefighters mounted, and, in 1948, Bastard Otto Friedli broke from the club and created the Hell's Angels Motorcycle Club in Fontana, California.

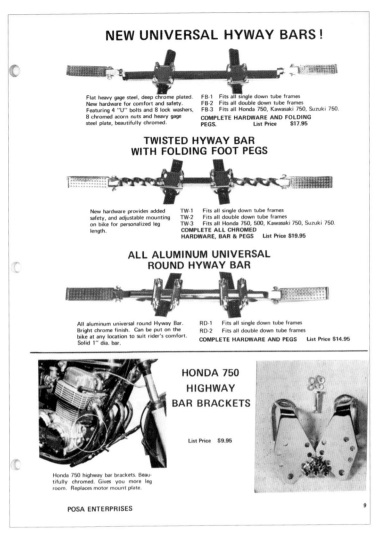

{ORGAN PIPES MAKE A STATEMENT:
THIS IS NO WEEKEND-WARRIOR BIKE.}

Through the late 1940s and early 1950s, the Hell's Angels continued to ride with the other ninety-nine percent, but already their reputation roared out in front. In 1954, the year Marlon Brando starred in *The Wild One*, the original Hell's Angels chapter merged with San Francisco's Market Street Commandos to spawn the club's second chapter, whose president crafted the intimidating winged death's head that remains the Hell's Angels calling card today.

{AMERICAN BIKES ARE OFTEN CHOPPED, BUT HONDAS GET INTO THE ACT AS WELL.}

Hell's Angels Drug Trafficking Syndicate

Chapters quickly popped up along the California coastline, but there was no organization among the groups, no single vision. All of that changed, however, when Ralph

"Sonny" Barger helped establish the Oakland chapter. Under Barger's guidance, the Hell's Angels chapters came together, hammering out bylaws, codes of conduct, patches, colors, tattoos, and clubhouses. Ironically, this standardization only strengthened the myth of the outlaw biker. There were tales of mayhem, violence, and destruction, and those accusations of rape in Monterey in the early 1960s. That high-profile rape case, historians believe, marked the beginnings of an international drug trafficking syndicate. In order to pay legal bills, the legend goes, the Hell's Angels made a few drug deals, selling methamphetamines and entering for the first time the world of big-money narcotics. The Hell's Angels' defense, however financed,

was successful, and the rape suspects were acquitted. The case was the first in a long string of high-profile accusations, arrests, and acquittals (including the incident at the Rolling Stones concert, in which one Hell's Angel was arrested for the killing but was later acquitted), suggesting that either the Angels were slippery or that police liked to arrest them despite flimsy evidence. Likely, the truth involves a bit of both.

Like the motorcycle manufacturers, organized outlaw clubs (and the Hell's Angels in particular) worked hard to clean up their media image. From a West Coast phenomenon of like-minded roustabouts, outlaw clubs became an iron and leather culture recognizable worldwide. In the late 1980s, journalist Yves Lavigne numbered

{LIGHTNING STRIKES WHEN-EVER THE KEY IS TURNED.}

the Hell's Angels at about one thousand full-time members in sixty-seven chapters in thirteen countries on four continents. But the loners and barroom toughs who characterized the club's early days in California were becoming an organized crime and drug syndicate, complete with high-tech communication and computer hardware. The savvy media manipulators who stage annual Toys for Tots drives bear little resemblance to the inarticulate Okies chronicled by Thompson and others in the 1960s.

The Hell's Angels incorporated, trademarked the death's head, and organized chapters around the world. Their boldness irritated law enforcement, and in the late 1970s and early 1980s, the U.S. government tried to pin an official organized crime designation on the group, hoping to prosecute the Hell's Angels under laws originally designed to combat the Mafia. The accusations of racketeering, influence, and corrupt organization laws were never proven, however, with two hung juries unable to come to a decision on thirty-eight of forty-four separate charges.

The 15 million dollar federal prosecution resulted in two mistrials, which prosecutors decried as a miscarriage of justice, while Sonny Barger threw a no-holds-barred bash for the jurors. Despite the verdict exonerating the motorcycle club, police in the U.S. and overseas continue

to consider the Hell's Angels a wealthy corporation with a global drug distribution network.

The Angels continue to deny all charges, and in 1998 happily celebrated their fiftieth anniversary. The Angels insist that if they were as bad as police allege, they would've been jailed and disbanded years ago. Their argument goes something like this: with such easy prey (Hell's Angels do, after all, advertise their affiliation with emblazoned colors), police must be either incompetent investigators or simply working under mistaken assumptions.

A Word from the Rivals

The Outlaws Motorcycle Club is one of the chief rivals of the Hell's Angels, and is the largest "one percent" motorcycle club in the world. Formed in Joliet, Illinois, in 1935, the Outlaws have approximately two hundred chapters in the United States, Canada, Australia, Asia, and Europe. U.S. chapters account for around two thousand members and European chapters about eight hundred. The Outlaws headquarters is Daytona Beach, Florida.

Each chapter has a clubhouse. These clubhouses are used for "church meetings," parties, and private gatherings. They are usually secured by concrete walls, steel doors, razor wire, guard dogs, and video surveillance.

Membership in the Outlaws is limited to men who own American-made motorcycles of a particular size, although in Europe motorcycles from any country are allowed, so long as they are in the chopper style. A prospective member is first a "hang-around" or associate. After having proven himself worthy, he is promoted to "probate" status and finally becomes a patched member.

A patched member is entitled to wear a leather or denim vest bearing an Outlaws emblem, called "colors." The patch is surrounded by chapter and club membership information, called "rockers." These emblems are purchased directly from the international president. A patched member is

also allowed to attend the weekly church meetings, while associates, pro-
bates, and "old ladies" wait outside. After being a member in good stand-
ing for a year, an Outlaw may get a tattoo depicting the Outlaws emblem.

An Outlaws tattoo can reflect other membership information as well.
An Outlaw who commits murder, attempts murder, or explodes a bomb
on behalf of the Outlaws may wear "lightning bolts," a Nazi-style SS tattoo. An Outlaw who has spent time in jail may receive an "LL" tattoo,
which stands for "Lounge Lizard."

While the Outlaws are allied with the Bandidos, a Southwestern
motorcycle club, they have rivalries with several other clubs. Their dislike of Hell's Angels is expressed in their slogans "AHAMD," or "All Hell's
Angels Must Die," and "ADIOS," or "Angels Die in Outlaws States." They
also dislike the Pagans and the Warlocks.

The Outlaws collect information on their rivalries with other clubs.
They primarily collect newspaper clippings regarding incidents with
other clubs. On occasion, though, an Outlaws member will bribe a law
enforcement officer to obtain information on the location of a rival club's
members. Outlaws also travel, at the club's direction, to the funerals of
fellow bikers.

{THE FLAMING SKULL
COMBINES TWO OF THE
MOST POPULAR IMAGES
IN CHOPPER ART.}

{OTHER POPULAR IMAGES INCLUDE EAGLES AND THE FLAG.}

A Brotherhood Against Totalitarian Enactments (ABATE). Not every pack
of bikers has looked to push back against the Man through illegal
activities. Back in June of 1971, a new and exciting motorcycle publication was introduced—*Easyriders*, a motorcycle magazine for the
entertainment of adult bikers.

Around this same time, an organization called the National Custom Cycle Safety Institute (NCCSI) also emerged. This organization was for manufacturers and distributors, and its main function
was to create safety standards for custom parts. It concentrated
mainly on custom front ends and frames with raked necks. The
NCCSI is credited for keeping a lot of junk off the market and pre-
venting over-regulation of parts.

In issue no. 3, October 1971, *Easyriders* started a nonprofit organization just for bikers. It was called National Custom Cycle Association (NCCA). Dues were three dollars for a one-year membership.
Back in 1971, no other motorcycle magazine except Roger Hall's
Road Rider gave even an inch of space to anti-bike legislation.

Before long, the NCCA was changed to ABATE (A Brotherhood
Against Totalitarian Enactments). ABATE used an eagle logo from
an old Civil War publication. The eagle is one of the largest birds
and a strong flier, and has long been used as a sign of power, courage, and freedom.

In 1972, ABATE started using area coordinators in different
states to help organize bikers so that they could better represent
ABATE on the local level. This also helped form a better line of communication. From this mushroomed a sophisticated network of state
and county chapters.

With its limited funds, ABATE hired an engineering firm to
determine whether a raked front end or an extended front end was
safer. Two lengthy, documented reports, complete with engineering drawings, established proof that both were safe. This enabled
bikers to fight "unsafe vehicle" tickets in court with scientific facts,

states. Each region has a regional coordinator to handle information between the state ABATE organizations.

{A HAND-PAINTED TANK GIVES THE FINAL TOUCH TO MAKE A BIKE YOUR OWN. }

not just opinions. From 1971 to 1974, most of ABATE's efforts went into fighting such laws. Had it not been for the efforts of this group in the early 1970s, choppers would have been outlawed.

In March of 1977, ABATE held a state coordinators meeting in Daytona, Florida. Attendees enacted a policy that ABATE, as a lobbying organization, would discourage back patches on cut-offs nationwide in order not to be misjudged as a club, either by outlaw groups, police, or citizens. Attendees also decided that ABATE should organize, with a charter, bylaws, and so on. Nominations were held, and five state coordinators were elected as a steering committee to take ideas from all the members and chapters and boil the results down to a charter and bylaws. The new steering committee was given seven months to get everything together.

At the next meeting, a disagreement between the people who worked for *Easyriders* and the state coordinators for ABATE led to a split in the ABATE organization. Two national organizations were formed: one in Sacramento, the other in Washington, D.C. However, the D.C. organization was soon dismantled and the leaders decided to dissolve the national organization altogether. Now the state ABATE groups could return to doing the business they were formed to do—fight state antimotorcycle legislation. ABATE formed five regional groups, each region comprising about ten

{THE COLONIAL FLAG ON THIS TANK IS DESTINED FOR A CHOPPER IN MASSACHUSETTS}

{ONE MIRROR, TWO PIPES.}

THE
LIFE

{SIMPLE MEN LIKE THIS TURNED STURG
DAYTONA INTO BURGEONING BIKER STO

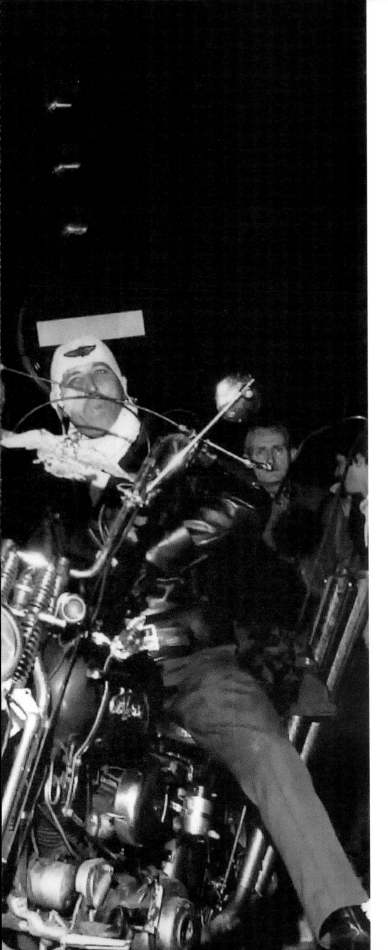

{Buying the Bike's Image}

In a stroke of marketing genius, Willy Davidson (of Harley-Davidson) mainstreamed the outlaw biker image by borrowing styling cues from the stripped-down choppers preferred by motorcycle gangs. Since the early 1990s, the outlaw biker image has been the dominant fashion model for motorcycling, and the trappings of the outlaw biker counterculture have been bowdlerized and co-opted by otherwise respectable motorcyclists. Not coincidently, interest in motorcycles has grown dramatically since 1990, with double-digit sales increases for nearly every manufacturer. Every marketing angle is now being explored to tap into the outlaw biker fantasy. The Hell's Angels themselves market Big Red, their own brand of custom motorcycles, and replicas of the choppers ridden in *Easy Rider* sell for more than $25,000. Motorcycle advertising frequently encourages consumers to abandon social conformity and celebrate the suppressed barbarian. An advertisement for mufflers, for instance, shows a leather-clad, tattoo-covered biker emerging from a three-piece suit with the line, "Inside every good guy there's a real bad ass." Other advertisements encourage bikers to "Raise some hell," or they pose the question, "Who cares where you are going?" or they remind the man that "You've got the attitude" or inspire him to "Take the low road." A Harley-Davidson motorcycle advertisement brags, "That's not Silicone, Friend"; no company has been more aggressive than Harley-Davidson in capitalizing on outlaw biker chic. You can even order a nihilistic factory paint scheme featuring grinning skulls. The company licenses beer, dolls, cloths, bed sheets, dishes, knives, watches, and shoes; even Christmas decorations now sport the black-and-orange Harley logo.

While the genuine outlaw biker still exists, the outlaw image has gone mainstream. Men love the media-made image of the biker: a do-rag-wearing, unshaven man roaming the streets of America on the back of his trusty steel steed. The weekend riders follow the real outlaw bikers to the same party spots and celebrations, wanting to feel like a rebel just for a little while.

{WHAT STARTED OUT AS A ONE-MAN OPERATION SOON GREW INTO A CORPORATION.}

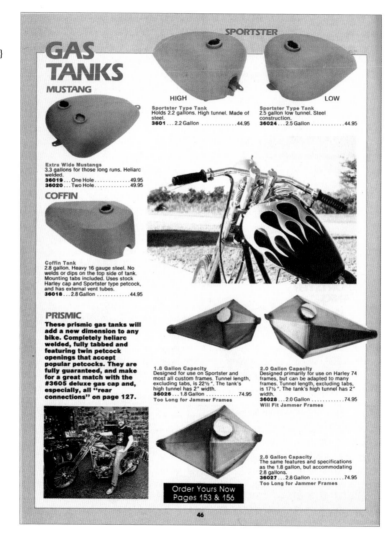

Sturgis

One of the largest modern-day celebrations of choppers and the outlaw image takes place at Sturgis, South Dakota. Every August, thousands of motorcycle riders, ranging from bikers to outlaws to enthusiasts, roll into town for a week.

The Sturgis Rally began in 1938 when J. C. "Pappy" Hoel, a local motorcycle shop owner, and some friends held a motorcycle race and stunt competition. The first event consisted of nineteen racers at the half-mile track and some dangerous events such as board-wall crashes, ramp jumps, and head-

{JUST ADD WATER?}

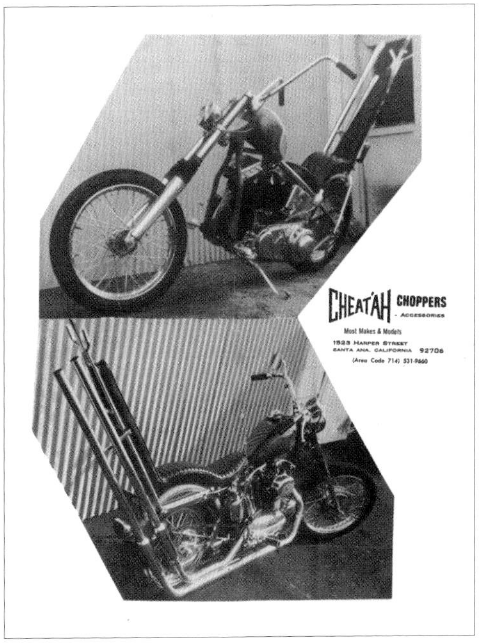

{YOU'VE GOT TO HAVE A BIG RIDE TO STAND OUT AT STURGIS.}

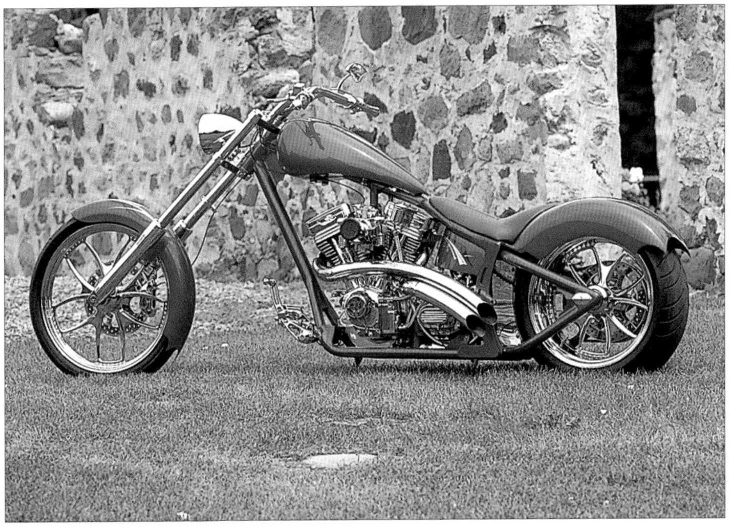

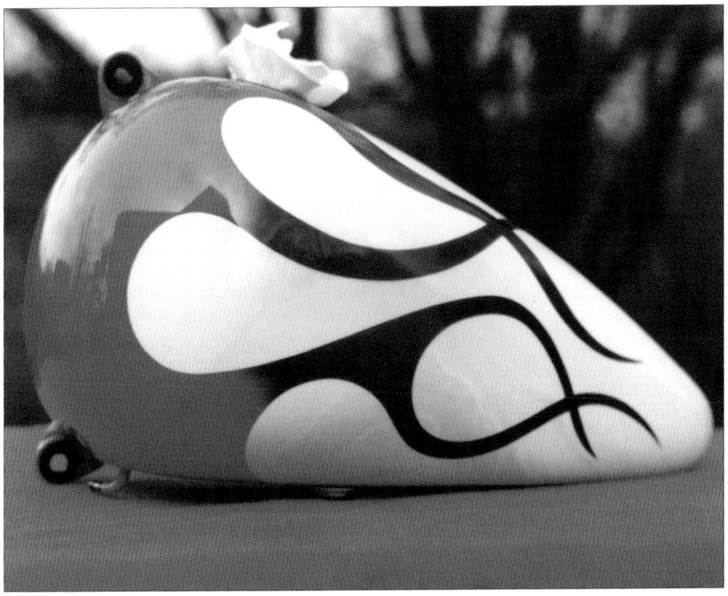

{HUNDREDS OF TANK ARTISTS WORK AT STURGIS AND DAYTONA.}

on collisions with cars. Local businesses put up $500 in prize money. The event was cancelled for a few years during World War II, but after the war, it grew as the motorcycling lifestyle gained popularity. One thousand motorcyclists attended the program in the city park during the 1965 rally. By the time the 1980s rolled around, attendance had climbed into the tens of thousands. For the Fiftieth Anniversary in 1990, approximately 400,000 bikers came to celebrate. In 1999, the event drew nearly 290,000 people from around the world. The biggest rally of all happened at the Sixtieth Anniversary in 2000, when estimated attendance was almost 633,000.

Sturgis is as close to an annual bikers convention as they come, and it is a pure celebration of motorcycling. People get together because they like bikes, but being a motorcycle enthusiast is only part of the equation. Motorcycling for attendees is more than a sport and more than a hobby. It's a state of mind. When people gather at the rally, sure they talk shop, but they also break away from the treadmill of everyday life.

Sturgis is a special place for motorcyclists. Steeped in history and situated in the scenic Black Hills, it offers serious scenery

{THE PARTY MAY NOT BE AS ROWDY AS IT USED TO BE, BUT BIKES LIKE THIS ARRIVE BY THE DOZENS.}

CAPTION?

{UNLIKE THE CATALOGUES OF OLD, YOU CAN PICK UP THE PARTS ON SITE.}

{MODERN SEATS ARE GUARAN-TEED TO FIT THEIR BIKES.}

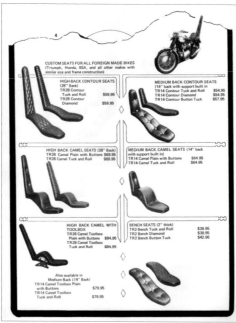

and solitude, with popular rides heading out to the Badlands, over to Devil's Tower in Wyoming, or past Sylvan Lake. Of course, a visit to Sturgis would not be complete without a trip down the historic Main Street. Five blocks are open to motorcycle traffic only, creating a sea of bikes and people. Astride their iron horses, people ride up and down the street, seeing the sights and being seen. There are colorful people and bikes, even one that looks like a buffalo. Vendors set up in the downtown area, selling a vast array of leather goods, T-shirts, tattoos, Internet services, jewelry, bike parts, and food.

Racing, the sport that started it all, remains an integral part of the event. Initially, the event began with a half-mile race, and there are half-mile races held today in both Sturgis and Rapid City. The rally also includes ADBA drag racing at Sturgis Dragway, as well as professional and amateur hill climbs at Bessie's Knob Hill.

Touring was not an original event at the rally, but it joined the event line-up within a few years. The first tours departed from Main Street and included everyone that attended the event. These days, tours are still a great way to experience the sites in the Black Hills. The "Dark of the Moon" tour takes people to Mount Rushmore for the evening lighting ceremony. The annual Governor's Tour brings many dignitaries to Sturgis for a ride to Mount Rushmore and the Crazy Horse monument.

{A FAT BOB TANK IS WIDER THAN A NORMAL TANK.}

[THE COLOR ISN'T THE ONLY
THING THAT MAKES ONLOOKERS
ENVIOUS.]

On February 24, 1947, the famous motorcycle race resumed and was now promoted by the legendary Bill France. Newspaper stories of the period recount that the city fathers asked townsfolk to open their homes to the visiting motorcyclists because all hotel rooms and camping areas were filled to capacity. The 1947 Daytona 200 featured a record 176 riders.

From 1948 through 1960, a new beach/road course was used because of developments along the beach. Organizers were forced to move the event farther south, towards Ponce Inlet. The new circuit measured 4.1 miles. In 1961, the famous race was moved to the Daytona International Speedway.

Vendors set up in the down-town area, selling a vast array of leather goods, T-shirts, tattoos, Internet services, jewelry, bike parts, and food.

Bike Week: Ride-Hard, Die-Free. Bike Week has always had a flavor of its own. Some time after the war, the event began to take on a rugged edge. While the motorcycle races on the beach were organized, events surrounding the race were not. As time passed, locals became afraid of the visitors, and law enforcement officers and city officials were less than enthusiastic about what some

Daytona and Bike Week

The Daytona 200. Perhaps it was the appeal of hard sand, and warm winter days that made Daytona Beach, Florida, the home of Bike Week. Maybe it is the spirited activities surrounding the event that keep people keep coming back. Whatever the case, Bike Week has been a tradition since January 24, 1937, the inaugural running of the Daytona 200.

The first race took place on a 3.2-mile beach and road course south of Daytona Beach. Ed Kretz of Monterey Park, California, was its first winner, riding an American-made Indian motorcycle and averaging 73.34 mph. Kretz also won the inaugural City of Daytona Beach trophy.

The races continued from 1937 to 1941. In the early years the Daytona 200 was also called the "Handlebar Derby" by local racing scribes.

The Daytona 200 was discontinued in 1942 because of World War II, but people still showed up for an unofficial party called Bike Week.

{NOT EVERYONE THAT RIDES A CHOPPER IS A COWBOY.}

{THE GRIP STYLING IS FOR BETTER CONTROL.}

{WHAT ON THE HIGHWAY TO HELL?}

termed an "invasion." Relations between the bikers and law enforcement officials continued to decline. After the 1986 event, a special task force was organized by the city in cooperation with the local chamber of commerce to improve relations and change the magnitude and scope of the event.

Today, Bike Week has evolved into a ten-day festival celebrated throughout Volusia County. Pilgrims from around the world come to Bike Week, the largest gathering of believers on the planet. The size of the event is unprecedented, colossal—six hundred thousand participants in 2000—and every motel, hotel, condo, campground, and fish camp within fifty miles is booked solid. Parking lots everywhere overflow with motorcycles. This revel boasts the most people, the most arrests, the most dead (fifteen in 2000), and the most alcohol consumed. As with other rites of reversal past and present, some form of intoxicant that reduces inhibitions is crucial. Imagine this: during any other ten-day period Boot Hill Saloon might sell two hundred cases of beer. During Bike Week 1999, that number rose to 8,300 cases. Along with a tolerance for public drunkenness, local prohibitions regarding decency, modesty, and safety are relaxed to allow a screw-the-world-style fantasy.

Horrified locals, law enforcement agencies, and emergency services brace themselves for the March invasion. (The Halifax County Hospital, for example, prohibits time off during the event.) "Deadly Week," shouts the 11 March 2000 *Daytona News-Journal*, with a two-inch headline, "The Bloodiest on Record." Alarmed editorialists write about noise, traffic, drunkenness, nudity, and criminal behavior—all of which, they argue, seem to slip closer to total anarchy with each passing year. "Boobs, bellies, and beards," one grumbles. "[We can't] sleep through the night without being awakened by a piercing blast." In truth, for ten days the rumble of motorcycles goes on twenty-four hours a day as the biker crowd jams the town to the bursting point. Near

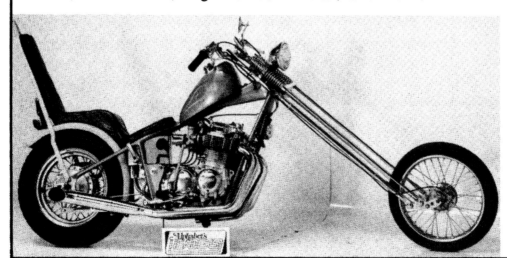

{CHOPPERS AND THE PEOPLE
THAT RIDE THEM.}

For Your
Viewing
Pleasure

the beach, traffic is often gridlocked, while along Main Street, the concentrated core of the event, crowds stand elbow to elbow to gawk at the endless, thundering parade of motorcycles of every conceivable color and decorative motif, including flames, cartoon characters, animals, nudes, sorcerers, dragons, and death heads.

The prominent costume, commonly associated with the outlaw biker, is black leather. Black leather boots, pants, chaps, jackets, hats, belts, bras, and vests are ubiquitous. (The color black, incidentally, represents the absence of light and has archetypal associations with evil and wickedness.) While the few participants who are actual motorcycle gang members—the fashion aristocracy here—wear their colors, most Bike Week leather merely mimics the outlaw biker costume by sporting advertisements for a particular brand of motorcycle and perhaps patches and pins available at bars and shops. The T-shirts, usually black, often sport skulls, snakes, saloons, vulgar messages, or manufacturers' logos. Silver jewelry, large and numerous rings, bracelets, wallet chains, and boot chains are *de rigueur* for communicating the sexy and menacing outlaw biker style.

The central icon of the event and the requisite accessory, of course, is the motorcycle. The "mystical relationship" that

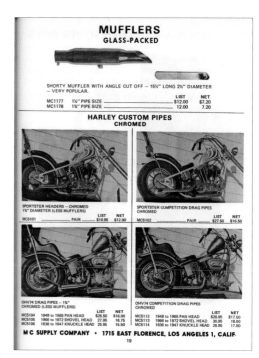

the biker has with his motorcycle is readily apparent during Bike Week. Most of the motorcycle owners, for example, have replaced quiet exhaust systems with louder, often earsplitting, after-market pipes. Bikers argue that being loud saves lives, but it is also conveniently exhibitionistic, the power of additional decibels enhancing the power the machine embodies. Beyond the satisfaction of thundering from one partying venue to another on a motorcycle, riders enjoy biking events everywhere: club

reunions; brand get-togethers; and contests for best American, British, or Italian bikes; best customs; biggest, smallest, oldest, and rattiest bikes.

As the focal point of the Bike Week hell-bent, lead-and-leather fantasy, the motorcycle is also the centerpiece of daring exploits and destructive celebrations. Bikers roar out of parking lots or, less commonly, pop wheelies on their 600-pound machines. Crowds gather for the popular Wall of Death daredevils like Rhett Rotten, who rides without hands twenty feet high on the rim of a huge wooden barrel to grab dollar bills from onlookers. Racing at the International Speedway culminates with the Daytona 200, where motorcycles rocket around the banked track at 200 mph. Huge crowds cheer wildly (and imagine they're participating in a patriotic rally) at ceremonial "bike drops," in which "Jap rice burners" are violently smashed and torched. In the burnout pits, particularly bold or intoxicated bikers rev their motorcycles through the gears, filling the air with acrid, black smoke as they burn off the rear tire, the cheers of the crowd lost in the earsplitting staccato from the red-hot engine.

{SHORT DRAG PIPES GIVE THIS BIKE A GROWL THAT WOULD SCARE ANY ANIMAL.}

Fueling all this drunken revelry are the most famous biker honky-tonks in the world: Boot Hill Saloon, Iron Horse Saloon, Dirty Harry's, Last Resort, and the Cabbage Patch—and there are a dozen other lesser-known biker hangouts throughout the county. Mostly empty during the year, they are jammed for Bike Week; and each day until late into the bonfire-illuminated nights, free rock-and-roll concerts feature thirty-five-year-old music to transport "outlaw" baby boomers back to their youth.

Undeniably, Bike Week includes a strong sexual focus. In fact, it is probably the most sexually charged public revel in existence. The motorcycle itself is powerfully phallic and certainly provides one explanation for the machine's profound allure and the unusually raucous character of Bike Week.

The relatively few women who attend Bike Week provide a focus for the display of machismo and, not surprisingly, the competitions for women are designed to objectify and celebrate female sexuality. There are Miss Budweiser, Miss Jim Beam, and Miss Bike Week contests. Nearly naked women wrestle in pudding, creamed corn, and coleslaw. Other contests award prizes for the biggest breasts, best breasts, hottest buns, best topless dancing, and most beautiful nude body. In these salacious spectacles, enthusiastic women are cheered and ogled by appreciative crowds of mostly middle-

{THIS PANHEAD PINUP RODE ALONGSIDE NUBILE BEAUTIES OF BIKER MAGAZINES.}

aged men, who no doubt relish the opportunity for fantasies of sexual prowess and license. Bike Week gluttony manifests itself nearly everywhere, and for this modern carnival one must pay a high price to flaunt propriety. Bike Week is an orgy of spending, a whopping $320 million in 1999, and hundreds of itinerant vendors sell every conceivable carnival accessory. At what other event could Camel Cigarettes merchandise lighters, cigarettes, and, of course, boot shines by buxom women?

The most popular foods of Bike Week also reflect the intemperate nature of the affair. Four-pound steaks, three-pound pork chops, smoked turkey legs, and huge fried sausages smothered in onions are washed down with thousands and thousands of gallons of beer, often peddled by bikini-clad women who pull cold cans from ice-filled garbage pails. (These positions, incidentally, are prized because the women typically earn more than $2,000 in tips.)

During Bike Week, imagery and rituals of subversion and nihilism abound, creating a context for acting out a ride-hard, die-free fantasy.

{THIS BIKE EMBODIES BOBBER ESSENCE WITH CHOPPER STYLE.}

{MAG WHEELS OFFER A SOLID RIDE.}

It Ain't Like It Used to Be

Having fun is serious business, and the current boom in motorcycling evidences the popularity of the outlaw biker fantasy. Bike Week is not the only motorcycle rally that is exploding in size, and new venues are springing up all over the country. Arizona now has its own Bike Week, and there are the huge new Laughlin, Nevada, carnival, and the Myrtle Beach revel in South Carolina. Like Daytona's Bike Week, all feature drinking and feasting, boisterous crowds, loud motorcycles, and the requisite symbols of outlawry, hedonism, and nihilism.

Demographers studying the size and constitution of the Bike Week crowds might conclude that interest in such affairs is faddish, that it is but another symptom of an affluent baby-boom generation's uncomfortable transition to midlife. And trend analysts predict that the decade-long motorcycle fad has just about run its course. There's some truth to both opinions, and perhaps the size of these events may erode. However, the source of Bike Week's popularity is more complex and resonates more deeply than a midlife crisis, and unless the motorcycle is simply outlawed as too dangerous for modern society, Bike Week and events like it will continue to thrive.

During Bike Week, imagery and rituals of subversion and nihilism abound, creating a context for acting out a ride-hard, die-free fantasy. For ten days, participants are allowed to show the world what they think of themselves and the world around them, and for many this means assuming the exaggerated masculinity of the "peacock" male in one of its most outrageous contemporary manifestations—the outlaw biker. For all of its sound and fury, however, the flaunting of anti-establishment attitudes during Bike Week is primarily symbolic fantasy, and with each passing year a growing burden of tradition continues to formalize the affair. Bike Week is narcissistic theater, a uniquely modern and American version of an experience that is

{THE FAT REAR TIRE AND DRAGSTER-STYLE FRAME SHOW YOU FOR WHAT THIS BIKE IS INTENDED.}

Photos by Bill Storm

{THIS VINTAGE BIKE IS WHERE THE "FACTORY CUSTOM" GOT SOME OF ITS IDEAS.}

At what other festival could Camel Cigarettes offer boot shines by buxom women?

probably as old as civilization itself. Accordingly, when it is over, most of the six hundred thousand "outlaws" suppress antisocial inclinations and return to lives of middle-class conformity and respectability.

As our society becomes more crowded and complex, more competitive and controlled, the inevitable result will be even higher levels of frustration and psychic suffering. Such pressure will manifest itself as a fascination with forbidden things that will become more extreme, and acts of hedonistic rebellion will become more frequent. Twenty years ago, before interest in Bike Week skyrocketed, popular festivals relaxing public order and established standards of decency were flourishing throughout the world. If the Bike Week–style revel is any indication, reversal rituals are becoming longer, more decadent, more difficult to control, and more lucrative. Such realities suggest that the oppressive burden of modern life is taking its toll.

{THIS BIKE IS READY TO TAKE ANY CHECKERED FLAG.}

GLOSSARY

(DRAG BARS: LOW, FAT, STRAIGHT HANDLEBARS.)

AMA: American Motorcycle Association

APE HANGERS: High handlebars that put a biker's hands at or above shoulder height

BACKYARD: Where you ride often

BAFFLE: Sound-deadening material that sits inside a muffler and quiets the exhaust note

BLOCKHEAD: The V-Twin engine Harley produced from 1984 to 2000

BONEYARD: Salvage yard for used bikes and parts

BRAIN BUCKET: Small, beanie-style helmet (usually not DOT approved)

BURNOUT: Spinning the rear wheel while holding the front brake

CAGE: Any non-motorcycle vehicle.

CAGER: Automobile driver

CHOPPER: Bike with the front end raked out or extended out

CHROMEITIS: Someone who just cannot get enough aftermarket accessories (especially chrome) is said to have Chromeitis

CHURCH: Clubhouse

CLAP: Chrome, Leather, Accessories, Performance

CLONE: A motorcycle built to resemble and function like a Harley-Davidson motorcycle without actually being one (the vehicle's title will identify it as something other than a Harley-Davidson)

COLORS: Motorcycle Backpatch

CRASH BAR: Engine Guard

CREDITGLIDE: RUB's Motorcycle

CROTCH ROCKET: Sport bike

COUNTER STEERING: Turning the bike's handlebars in one direction and having it go in the opposite direction

CUSTOM: Custom-built bike

CUT: Vest with club colors

DOT: Department of Transportation

DRAG BARS: Low, flat, straight handlebars

EVO / EVOLUTION®: The Evolution engine (V-Twin, produced from 1984 to 2000)

FATHEAD: The twin-cam engine (V-Twin, produced from 1999 to the current day)

FLATHEAD: The Flathead engine (V-Twin, produced from 1929 to 1972)

FLASH PATCH: Generic patches usually sold at swap meets and shops

FLYING LOW: Speeding

FORWARD CONTROLS: Front pegs, shifter, and rear brake control toward the front of the bike so the rider can stretch out his legs

HARD TAIL: A motorcycle frame with no rear suspension

HOG: Harley Owner's Group

INDEPENDENT: Someone who is not a part of any club or group, but is part of the biker culture

INK: Tattoo

INK-SLINGER: Tattoo artist

KNUCK/KNUCKLEHEAD: The Knucklehead engine (V-Twin, produced from 1936 to 1947)

LE/LEO: Law Enforcement/Law Enforcement Officer

LEAVING YOUR MARK: Oil puddle on the ground where you parked your scoot

M/C: Motorcycle Club

MSF: Motorcycle Safety Foundation

OEM: Original Equipment Manufacturer

ONE PERCENTERS: If you read the papers or listen to the news, the media and law enforcement agents have redefined the term one percenters. Term was first used in the '60s to describe bikers who were hard riding, hard partying, free-spirited type people (that is, one percent of the riding population—the other ninety-nine percent belonged to mainstream society). Some of the early bikers embraced the term, feeling it distinguished them as men who rode their motorcycles seven days a week in all kinds of weather, and liked to drink and raise a little hell. Sometime during the '80s, however, the meaning changed to "law-breaking lowlifes," at least in the eyes of law enforcement and the media.

PAN/PANHEAD: The Panhead engine (V-Twin, produced from 1948 to 1965)

PILLION PAD: The passenger seat

PIPES: Exhaust system

PLUGS: Spark plugs

PUCKER FACTOR: Refers to how tight your ass got on a close call

R/C: Riding Club

RAGS: Also used to refer to cut or colors

RAT BIKE: An older bike that doesn't look like it has been taken care of at all

REVOLUTION™: The Revolution engine, Harley-Davidson's first water-cooled engine (V-Twin, produced from 2002 to the current day)

RICO: Racketeer Influenced and Corrupt Organizations; laws passed to combat organized crime (such as the Mafia) that are also used against motorcycle clubs

RIDIN' BITCH: Riding as passenger

ROCKER: The part of motorcycle colors that designate geographic location or territory

RUB: Rich Urban Biker

RUBBER: Tire

RUBBER SIDE DOWN: Ride safe; don't crash the bike

RUN: Road trip with your buds, most of the time with a destination in mind

SCOOT: Motorcycle

{A V-TWIN, EVOLUTION ENGINE.}

{SOME BIKES SUFFER FROM CHROMEITIS.}

{NOTE THE IRON CROSS ON THE SISSYBAR.}

{THIS BIKE RIDES ON THE EDGE.}

SHINY SIDE UP: Ride safe; don't lay the bike down

SHOVEL/SHOVELHEAD: The Shovelhead engine (V-Twin, produced from 1966 to 1984)

SISSY BAR: Passenger backrest

SLAB: Interstate

SLED: Motorcycle

SOFTAIL®: A motorcycle frame whose suspension is hidden, making it resemble a hard tail

STRAIGHT PIPES: An exhaust system with no baffles

TATS: Tattoos

TAIL GUNNER: The last rider in a group

THIRTEEN (13): Patch commonly worn by outlaw bikers; can have several meanings, the most common of which is "marijuana" or "meth" (since M is the thirteenth letter in the alphabet). Thirteen also stands for the original, or "mother," chapter of a motorcycle club. In the last few years, many places have begun saying the M stands for motorcycle. In the "ESE" or Mexican community, the number thirteen is often used to represent the "South Side" and "La Eme" (Mexican Mafia)

TURN YOUR BACK: To completely disassociate from a person or club

TWISTIES: Section of road with a lot of turns

WANNABE: Someone who tries to be a part of the biker lifestyle

WRENCH: Mechanic

XXF – FXX/XXFOREVER – FOREVERXX: Patch worn by motorcycle members to advertise their total commitment to the club and every member of that club (XX stands for the name of the club)

RAISE A LITTLE HELL. SOMETIME DURING THE '80S, HOWEVER, THE MEANING CHANGED TO "LAW-BREAKING LOWLIFES," AT LEAST IN THE EYES OF LAW ENFORCEMENT AND THE MEDIA.

INDEX